# Seeing
# with the
# Heart

**Other Books by Kevin O'Brien**

*The Ignatian Adventure: Experiencing the Spiritual Exercises of Saint Ignatius in Daily Life*

# Seeing
# with the
# Heart

## A Guide to Navigating
## Life's Adventures

## KEVIN O'BRIEN, SJ

LOYOLA PRESS.
A JESUIT MINISTRY
Chicago

LOYOLA PRESS.
A JESUIT MINISTRY

www.loyolapress.com

The poem "Ithaka," is from *C. P. Cavafy: Collected Poems*, Princeton University Press. Used by permission.
*Imprimi potest:* Very Rev. Joseph O'Keefe, SJ, Provincial

Cover art credit: vural/iStockphoto/Getty Images, Loyola Press
Back cover author photo: Fairfield University

ISBN: 978-0-8294-5529-8
Library of Congress Control Number: 2022945618

Printed in the United States of America.
24 25 26 27 28 29 30 31 SMN-Bang 10 9 8 7 6 5 4 3 2

For my parents,

whom you will meet in these pages.

In loving memory

and in gratitude

for teaching me so much about faith, hope,
and love.

"Here is my secret.

It's quite simple:

One sees clearly only with the heart. Anything essential is invisible to the eyes."

—Antoine de Saint-Exupéry, *The Little Prince*

# Contents

# Introduction

## The Adventure Continues

The adventure continues, but in different form.

In 2011, I published *The Ignatian Adventure: Experiencing the Spiritual Exercises of St. Ignatius in Daily Life*, a contemporary adaptation of the *Spiritual Exercises*, written by St. Ignatius of Loyola, founder of the Jesuits, nearly five hundred years ago. Ignatius crafted the Exercises during a period of his life when he experienced a profound transformation, both in his spiritual life and in his worldly commitments. Letting go of his ambitions to serve the royal court in Spain, he opted for a more itinerant and simple life. He described himself as a pilgrim, a familiar term in Ignatius's time, when pilgrimages to holy places were common. As Ignatius met people along the road, he talked to them about God and shared his Exercises, adapting them to meet each person's particular needs.

Ignatius had an experience of God, which he expressed through the Exercises, and these Exercises resonated widely. They have helped countless people over the centuries and across cultures to grow in faith, hope, and love and to make better decisions about their lives. *The Ignatian Adventure*, written in English and translated into Spanish, proposed a retreat based on the Exercises that could be made over a number of weeks in the midst of one's daily routine. In this book, I offer a different, broader approach to Ignatius's work by focusing on the tradition of spirituality that underlies and animates the Exercises.

A wise Jesuit friend once told me that tradition should act more like a rudder than an anchor. As an anchor, tradition can immobilize us, much like an anchor keeps a boat from moving down a flowing river. Unwilling to let go of old habits and ways of thinking, we cling to the past, usually out of fear or lack of imagination. We get stuck in one place and time, or in one way of thinking. In contrast, tradition as a rudder gives us something to hold on to, but it does not immobilize us. The past with its wisdom steers us along the river of history without dictating the shore where we will land. We are at play with the freedom of the river.

Similarly, the Ignatian tradition, expressed in the Spiritual Exercises, offers a rudder to guide us, allowing us to tack this way and that way, depending on what's happening in our lives. From his own experience, Ignatius believed that God works with each of us personally and uniquely. Respecting that privileged encounter, Ignatian spirituality is steeped in the wisdom of the past, attentive to the present context of each person, and open to the future. This spiritual tradition presumes that we, too, are pilgrims on a spiritual journey to God, with all its twists and turns, certainties and surprises. We are on the way to something or Someone greater than ourselves.

Rather than outlining a retreat as in the first book, here I present the key dimensions of our life as pilgrims, which find expression in Ignatius's Exercises. Each way of living builds on the other, beginning with the first:

1. Living with purpose
2. Living the questions
3. Living with depth
4. Living in freedom
5. Living out of great desires
6. Living with compassion
7. Living in hope
8. Living with discernment

The currents in our lives are sometimes smooth, sometimes rough. With the Ignatian tradition as our rudder, we can navigate them in a way that draws on their power to get us where we need to go.

I write with a diverse audience in mind: those with firm conviction in their faith and those who are struggling, those from the Christian tradition and those from other faith traditions, those who are actively religious and those who are seeking purpose and meaning in a less structured way. For the past few decades, Jesuits have expanded their efforts to share their spiritual and intellectual tradition with a wide audience. That tradition has been enriched by the wisdom and lived experience of women and men from a variety of backgrounds and cultures.

One of the most common phrases that we find in Ignatius's voluminous correspondence preserved today is "to help souls" or, as we would say today, to help people. It sounds basic, even obvious, but Ignatius did not want his Jesuits to get lost in abstractions. They were to stay focused on their fundamental mission—expressed in a variety of ministries—to help people in mind, body, and spirit. In doing so, they gave glory to God as much as when they said their prayers (which Ignatius also insisted on!). In this spirit, I hope this book is helpful to you as you strive to live more faithfully, hopefully, and lovingly, and to grow in your humanity. I hope what you read here will help you live more authentically, making decisions that reflect who you most truly are.

In keeping with the very practical dimension of Ignatian spirituality, I present some spiritual exercises at the end of each chapter that you can use to put into practice the central ideas of the reading. These exercises invite you to turn inward, to enrich your spiritual life but also to turn outward, to help others. You can revisit these short exercises after reading the book if you need a spiritual "tune-up," for the pilgrim life never really ends.

For Ignatius, the personal encounter between the human and the divine is conversational in nature. In contrast to the traditional view of God who commands our blind obedience, the God Ignatius met and whom he presents in the Spiritual Exercises is one with whom we can have a conversation. Ignatius took the same approach in his ministry, relying on conversation to accompany people and help them. The pilgrim does not walk alone. Following Ignatius's lead, imagine this book as an extended conversation that you and I are having about things that really matter to us. I bring into our conversation many of my favorite authors, artists, and poets. You may also extend this conversation to others in your life as you share with them what you learn here.

To keep the conversational flow of the narrative, I include source material for those writers and artists at the end of the book, instead of in footnote form. For ease, I include reference numbers to the *Spiritual Exercises*, our central text, in the narrative, indicated as SE, with the pertinent paragraph number. When I refer to the written text of the *Exercises*, I italicize the word, as is the practice in attributing written sources. However, when I refer to the Exercises as an experience, I do not italicize the word.

Not specifically attributed here are the many students I have taught over the years whose questions and comments in class and in their writing inspired my own thinking, praying, and imagining. They are the inspiration for this book. The Ignatian tradition speaks to a new generation, thank God.

Although I present some of my own experiences and lessons learned, my approach here is more invitation than imitation. God works with each of us so uniquely and personally in the complicated details of any human life that a standard or coerced approach to spirituality will not do. Instead, adapt the reading and exercises in ways meaningful for you. When I share stories, which I hope you can relate to, I have sometimes changed the names of persons and details to respect confidentiality.

I complete this book as we are emerging (please, God) from the worst of the COVID-19 pandemic, which began in early 2020. It will take years for us to really understand the multilayered impacts of this time and mourn our many losses. I do not dare now to put some final word on such a profound experience. While I offer no neatly wrapped lessons, insight might emerge in some form because writers do not write and readers do not read in a hermetically sealed vacuum, unaffected by their environment. I am changed—we are all changed—because of what we have gone through together.

Finally, in this book, you will hear frequently from Pope Francis, who is serving as pope while I have been writing. I rely on him because he speaks so much to my mind and heart about what my faith and my church is or should be about. He also speaks so clearly as a Jesuit who has given the Exercises to many people over his lifetime. His insights into the Spiritual Exercises and the Ignatian tradition of discernment are particularly valuable for us.

If we take the rudder confidently but lightly in hand, the currents will lead us to a shore where joy awaits. I do not mean happiness, which can be fleeting, even induced. Joy is a gift, and like love, it is a mystery, defying easy description. "Joy is not expressed the same way at all times in life, especially at moments of great difficulty," Pope Francis reminds us. "Joy adapts and changes, but it always endures, even as a flicker of light born of our personal certainty that, when everything is said and done, we are infinitely loved." Joy comes when we live out of the deepest sense of who we are, when we let **God and others come close, when we offer our lives in the service of others, when we rest in the stillness and beauty of our world. The shore where joy** awaits is shaped by the river we run. It may look different to each of us, but it is there, ready to welcome us.

# Chapter 1

# LIVING WITH PURPOSE

## Having the Experience and Not Missing the Meaning

I sat at my desk with piles of law books around me, one stacked on top of another, opened to pages that promised the winning argument our clients expected. I looked out my window, palm trees blowing in the wind, the Intracoastal Waterway in the distance. As much as I loved rummaging through pages hunting for the scent of a new insight that would change minds and shift opinions, I wanted to be outside in the Florida sun. More to the point, I realized I wanted to be outside the practice of law. I was restless for something different, something more. Around this time, Colleen, the principal of a local Catholic high school I had attended about a decade earlier, asked me after an advisory board meeting whether I ever thought about teaching. She had a position opening. The truth was that I *had* thought about teaching, but I declined her kind offer. *Who leaves a law practice to teach high school?*

Fast-forward a year, to another desk. This time in a high school classroom, papers to grade in neat piles. The thirty-five seats in front of me were empty, my students having had their fill of social studies for the day. Grading wasn't fun—any teacher will tell you that—but I was happy, and grateful that I had called Colleen back a few weeks later to accept the offer that I just couldn't get out of my mind. The lawyers at my firm kindly offered to keep my place at the firm open for a year, thinking I just needed to get this out of my system. The school was not far from my law office, and I even taught some of my former law partners' children. (This made parent-teacher conferences a bit odd at first!) I spent my days at the high school on my feet, teaching history and political science, and later religion. I loved the frenetic energy of students and the creativity and commitment of my fellow teachers. Having seldom kicked a soccer ball in my youth, I even agreed to coach the girls' team, which had lost its coach. I started a retreat program that would continue on long after I left. My days were full, and I went to bed each night with a good kind of tired.

I loved what I was doing. Yet I was still restless, even in my heart, having ended a long-term relationship about the same time I started teaching.

I was like so many twentysomethings, trying to figure out my life and impatient to get where I needed to go. The catch was this: I had no clear idea about what that destination was. I needed an Ithaka, the island home that Odysseus returned to after the siege of Troy in Homer's *Odyssey*. Odysseus knew where he wanted to go. I did not. Nor did I realize at the time the more important lesson that the journey is sometimes as important as the destination. In his modern take on the epic journey, the Greek poet C. P. Cavafy closed his poem "Ithaka" with this lesson in mind:

> Keep Ithaka always in your mind.
> Arriving there is what you're destined for.
> But don't hurry the journey at all.
> **Better if it lasts for years,**
> so you're old by the time you reach the island,
> wealthy with all you've gained on the way,
> not expecting Ithaka to make you rich.

Too immature to understand this lesson, and eager to get to the finish, I set my sights across the ocean, convinced I would find the meaning of life in Europe, like all romantics were supposed to do. I persuaded a childhood friend of mine to spend part of a summer backpacking across the continent. There, I was certain that I would meet someone or have *the* experience that would make my life's direction clear.

My summer escapade, though a lot of fun, was a fool's journey. When I returned home, the questions remained, my heart was still unsettled, and my lawyer-turned-teacher's bank account was considerably depleted. The American Buddhist nun and writer Pema Chödrön captures so well my quixotic searching. "Nothing ever goes away until it has taught us what we need to know," she writes in *When Things Fall Apart*. "If we run a hundred miles an hour to the other end of the continent in order to get away from the obstacle, we find the very same problem waiting for us when we arrive. It just keeps returning with new names, forms, and manifestations until we learn whatever it has to teach us."

Put another way, I fell into the trap that T. S. Eliot famously described in "The Dry Salvages," a poem in his *Four Quartets*: "We had the experience but missed the meaning." I thought that if I collected enough experiences, or at least had one very dramatic experience, my restlessness would cease and all would become clear. I was expecting to find the answers "out there" some-where, skipping the more difficult task of searching inside myself. I could collect like trophies a variety of interesting experiences and personal encoun-ters, but such scavenging does not automatically make meaning, and it usu-ally leads to emptiness and a fragmented life. To ensure that we do not miss the meaning in a frenetic race to the finish, we must live more purposefully.

In this chapter, I explore what it means to live with such purpose. Here is the good news that I was slow to understand: while frustrating at times, restlessness is part of being human and has a purpose—it animates and energizes us. Sure, if unchecked, restlessness can send us crashing against the shore, like a boat at the mercy of rough waters. Living with purpose, however, channels our restlessness, like a rudder navigating the currents to get us safely to our Ithaka. To live with purpose means that we pilgrims focus on our destination so that we stay on course while also paying atten-tion to our experience on the journey so that we can appreciate its meaning or beauty. In other words, we do as Cafavy urged us: keep Ithaka always in our mind, but without hurry to get there, because the journey has some-thing to teach us or reveal to us. Wisdom or insight unfolds, sometimes very gradually. Thankfully, life—or God—is a very patient teacher.

# Finding Your First Principle and Foundation

When I returned to Florida from my time of exploration in Europe, I got serious about my spiritual life. I began to appreciate the deep, holy desires that had governed my life in different measures depending on my maturity. My faith and my family instilled in me a duty to serve, to give back. As I got older, this duty turned into a heartfelt desire, animating my interest in public service in college and then law school. The desire to serve drove my decision to teach and took new shape in my emerging interest to serve as a priest. I loved the vibrantly crazy life of a high school teacher and coach, but I was wanting something more.

During this time, I learned to listen to God speaking to me through the people in my life: my family and friends, my fellow teachers and students, and even people I crossed paths with only briefly. As I reflected on my life, I found meaning in experiences whose significance I began to appreciate more and more. I remembered more vividly conversations with Jesuits while in college at Georgetown University, when my interest in becoming a Jesuit was initially sparked. I cherished as a gift an encounter I had with a client, Miriam, when practicing law. Miriam was a small Jewish woman from Brooklyn with a gentle spirit and strong convictions. Her case involved a will, a complicated and painful family history, and lots of land in Florida. She really did not care about the money; principle mattered most to her. As a young lawyer on the case, my primary responsibility was to take care of her, our client. One day in court, Miriam got upset and left the courtroom. I joined her as we walked around the courthouse block in the hot Florida sun. As we did, it hit me: *I would rather be talking to her than inside the courtroom!* This insight was not fleeting but significant. It stuck with me and made me open to leaving my law practice.

After returning from Europe, I took a radically honest look at my life, with all its beauty and brokenness. I understood better why a long-term relationship had ended as I made the transition to high school teaching; matters of the heart are rarely uncomplicated. My spiritual exploration also stirred my imagination, which helped me look at my future in new ways.

This interior journey, which I paint here in broad strokes, ultimately led me to apply to the Society of Jesus (more informally known as the Jesuits) when I was twenty-eight years old.

One of the qualities of the Jesuits that attracted me was their adventurous spirit. When St. Ignatius of Loyola founded the Jesuits in the 1500s, he insisted that their life be characterized by a generous availability. While other religious orders were tied to a certain location or type of ministry, Jesuits were to distinguish themselves by serving wherever the need was greatest, regardless of the location or the work. Our home is the road, an early Jesuit explained, capturing in a few words the lesson of the poem "Ithaka." Reflecting on his life, Ignatius referred to himself as a pilgrim. Contemporary statues of Ignatius fittingly depict him as a man in motion with a long walking stick firmly in hand, and one foot raised, stepping forward.

Ignatius's self-description as "pilgrim" emerged from his own life story. As a young man, he was restless. Ignatius thought that he would serve the Spanish royal court as a knight and nobleman. But after an injury in battle, and a long convalescence at his family's modest castle in the Basque Country of northern Spain, he began to reassess his life and put aside his youthful vanities. Once recuperated, Ignatius, the pilgrim, left his family and traveled across Europe and the Holy Land, still restless in his search for meaning. He talked to all sorts of people. He got some formal schooling. He spent extended times in solitude, listening more deeply to the movements of his soul. Along the way, Ignatius wrote down notes about how God was working with him, and he started sharing his experience with others who were interested in deepening their spiritual life. From these conversations with God and others, Ignatius crafted a book of exercises for the soul, a record of his spiritual journey that he thought would be helpful for others who were also pilgrims searching for God and meaning. This book, a guide for anyone's journey, is known today as the *Spiritual Exercises* of St. Ignatius.

The opening meditation of the Exercises, commonly titled "First Principle and Foundation," begins with these words: "Man is created to praise, reverence, and serve God our Lord, and by this means to save his soul" (SE 23). Ignatius then explains that we should be open to embracing whatever helps us achieve that end and let go of whatever gets in the way. In a later chapter, we will explore in more depth this stance of freedom, but for now, I highlight those opening words: we are created to praise, love, and serve God. By implication, this also means to love and serve others, because love of God and love of neighbor are inseparable, both part of the great commandment articulated by Jesus (Matthew 22:34–40). This is Ignatius's mission statement for the human person: we are created to know and love God and others. Everything we do or don't do should be weighed against that end.

On his journeys, Ignatius learned that God is laboring and waiting to be noticed by us in all sorts of people and places. Unless we pay attention and do the interior work of our head and heart, we are likely to miss God's divine presence. Unless we stay focused on our purpose—however we choose to define that end—we are likely to make choices that get us off course. What is secondary can easily become primary; what is a distraction becomes central.

Ignatius knew how easy it was to lose focus. Soon after leaving the family castle, he spent a year in the nearby town of Manresa, where his days were filled with prayer, service, and spiritual conversation. It was during this period that he began to write the *Spiritual Exercises*. At Manresa, Ignatius overcorrected himself, becoming scrupulous about his past sins and inflicting excessive penances on himself. He was plagued with doubts. His preoccupation dissolved any focus on loving God and others. Fear—in this case, of God's wrath—left no room for love. Eventually, through the counsel of trusted mentors, he began to understand what was happening inside him. He began to enjoy personal experiences of God's mercy and closeness to him. After a period of turmoil, Ignatius found peace and became zealous to continue his pilgrim journey.

# Staying Focused on Your End

In my first year as a Jesuit, I had my own "Manresa" experience. My fellow novices and I spent a month making the Spiritual Exercises at a retreat house on a beautiful piece of land on the Atlantic Ocean north of Boston. Being originally from Canada, I did not mind long walks in the cold

January coastal winds. Though surrounded by other retreatants, we spent most of the month in silence, except for our regular meetings with a spiritual director and going to Mass daily. The purpose of both the setting and the silence was to create an environment in which we could go deep and become better attuned to the movement of our souls.

A few days after completing the retreat, we headed to Mexico to live, study, and work for two months. Like the Spiritual Exercises, the pilgrimage experience was prescribed by Ignatius in the founding documents of the Jesuits. Its aim is to stretch young Jesuits, teaching them to rely more on God and the goodness of others in unfamiliar and often challenging circumstances. The transition from the solitude and silence of the retreat to the hectic pace and crowded living environment in Mexico was jarring, as different as the cold New England coast and subtropical Mexico.

I lived in a Jesuit community in the middle of a crowded barrio on a hill on the outskirts of Guadalajara, one of the poorest parts of the city. I shared a room with two Mexican scholastics who put up with my rudimentary Spanish. They were very patient with me. Case in point: for the first few weeks, I referred to myself as an avocado, mixing up the English word for the delicious ingredient of guacamole with *abogado*, the Spanish word for lawyer! Friday nights in the barrio were particularly noisy, with music blaring to mark the end of a long workweek. We recognized the futility of trying to sleep on those nights, so we passed the time happily on our rooftop patio, crossing cultures and language barriers as best we could. (Admittedly, the *cervezas* helped.)

Once I settled into my new environment, the primary task of my pilgrimage surfaced. It was pretty easy praying and reflecting in the tranquility of a month-long retreat on the Atlantic coastline. Much harder was to find a rhythm for reflecting amid the more chaotic and noisy life in Mexico. There, I was meant to apply the lessons and insights of the Spiritual Exercises to "real life," with all its complexity and unpredictability. I was having so many experiences, but without reflecting on them, I would miss their meaning. I was learning that Ignatian spirituality was very practical. For this reason, the first Jesuits—trying to explain themselves to those puzzled by their approach to religious life—referred to themselves as "contemplatives in action." I was really good at action, and gradually learning the contemplative part, but bringing those two together was an art I was just beginning to learn—and one that I continue to learn even now.

Connecting my spiritual or interior life with my active life of learning and ministry was especially critical when, after a month in Mexico, I faced a spiritual crisis. Like Ignatius in Manresa, I was racked by doubts. I kept thinking about all I had left in Florida seven months before when I joined the Jesuits. In the unfamiliar and sometimes frustrating surroundings of Mexico, I missed teaching very much and longed to see my friends and family. Frankly, I also missed the material comforts and predictable routine of home. I fretted about the future: *Would I be able to make it as a Jesuit whose home is the road?*

It got so bad that I wondered if I was even meant to be a Jesuit. These thoughts and an empty feeling in the pit of my stomach lingered just below the surface of my consciousness, popping up when I found time and space for quiet, especially as I fell asleep or awoke in bed. I decided to share these thoughts and feelings with my spiritual director, Gerry, when he visited from the States, even though I feared he would suggest that I leave the Jesuits. After patiently listening to my doubts and complaints, he smiled, clearly having seen this before in many Jesuit novices. "Kevin," he counseled, "focus on the present, not what you gave up in the past or what the Jesuits might ask you to do in the future. What is God showing you today?"

Distracted by fears and preoccupations, I had lost focus on my "first principle and foundation," which was to serve. I really loved meeting new people and learning the language and culture. I was amazed at the friendships I made across our differences. I also noticed how the bonds among my Jesuit classmates on pilgrimage were deepening. I embraced my time in Mexico less as a task and more as an invitation, even an adventure. My prayer came alive as I reflected on how the people and experiences were helping me grow in faith, hope, and love. My passion to enliven faith with justice was stirred up as I ministered with Mexican Jesuits in poor neighborhoods. This kind of honest reflection on my experience also presented me with some hard lessons about how captive I was to the materialism and individualism of my North American culture. Naming those traps was the first step to becoming free of them.

My fresh perspective made all the difference when I spent Holy Week at a small, rural village in the mountains outside of Guadalajara. I was dropped off by some Mexican Jesuit scholastics (that is, Jesuits in training) who traveled to a nearby village where they were staying. On my own, and fumbling with my Spanish, I was reliant on the kindness of the *campesinos.* One family took me into their home. Another made sure I was well fed. A group of young people included me in their preparations for a Good Friday procession through the village during which they would enact the stations of the cross, a living drama depicting Jesus' suffering and death. They enthusiastically invited me to play the role of Jesus. I'm embarrassed to say that after finding out that this role would require me to literally carry a cross and then stand on the upright cross for a couple of hours in the hot sun, I suggested that they ask one of the young men in the village to assume the coveted role. (So much for honoring the biblical exhortation to carry your cross daily!) The young people saw the wisdom of my self-serving suggestion and for my cowardice rewarded me with the role of Pontius Pilate.

My visit ended with an unforgettable Easter Vigil Mass. As darkness descended on the night before Easter Sunday, the people gathered in front of the church in the village square. High above, in the steeple of the church, a torch was lit and propelled down a wire to the center of the square, igniting a bonfire to symbolize the light of Christ coming into the darkness. On that night, as in the days before, there was more than enough in the present to ground me. Distractions about the past, or worry about the future, faded. Peace settled in.

A few weeks later, we returned to the United States, and our formation in the Jesuit way of life continued. As with any commitment, there were good days and bad days and lots of very ordinary days in between. The following year, I professed vows as a Jesuit, but that was only one signpost on the journey. I spent the next eight years in study and ministry as I prepared for ordination for the priesthood, living in different cities and countries for extended periods of time. My itinerant life has continued in the years since my ordination, a testament to enduring relevance of the age-old adage that our home is the road.

The road for me has usually been a source of blessing, not burden. In each place my religious superiors sent me, God blessed me with meaningful work and friendships, which helped me get through times of struggle and truly savor moments of joy. In the tougher moments, I have tried not to lose sight of my purpose, the mission I share with other Jesuits: to help souls, to love God and neighbor. That might be your purpose too, or maybe your purpose is something else: heaven, or a well-lived life, or a beloved community of friends and family, or infinite love, or all of those. Regardless of how we define our end, we keep that horizon in our view so that we do not get off course.

## Traveling the Distance Between Head and Heart

As adventurous as the road has been, the more challenging journey has been traveling the distance between my head and heart and truly becoming a contemplative in action, a reflective person amid activity. The words of the British novelist George Eliot ring true: "Adventure is not outside man; it is within." Key to connecting mind and heart and orienting me during the twists and turns of my life on the road has been the Spiritual Exercises. As I mentioned earlier, the pilgrim Ignatius jotted down insights from his own spiritual journey and fine-tuned them as he shared them with others. He did this not as a priest or a saint, but as a perceptive, curious, committed layperson searching for meaning and restless for a more fulfilling life.

I first encountered the Exercises in dramatic form: during those thirty days of silence on the Atlantic coast. But from their inception five centuries ago, Ignatius insisted that the Exercises should be adapted to daily life. He was a very practical man, more comfortable out on the streets of a city than in a monastery high in the mountains. Just as we need daily physical exercise to stay healthy, he wrote, so too does our soul (SE 1), and the Spiritual Exercises offer such a program for exercising and enlarging the soul. Fr. Arturo Sosa, SJ, superior general of the Jesuits, described the Exercises as "a pedagogy in how to communicate with God from the deepest part of ourselves, our affections." Thoughtfully, prayerfully, even courageously, we bring our mind, heart, and spirit into conversation with what we experience in our sometimes clear, sometimes confusing lives. We reflect on what is happening both around us and in us.

Ignatius's program is a distinctive school of the heart. We will delve further into the key movements of the Exercises in later chapters, but for now, it may be helpful to view the Exercises in broad outline, particularly if you are unfamiliar with them. We begin the Exercises by considering our mission, our principle and foundation, which orients us on the journey. We see more clearly what helps and hinders our realizing that mission. We meditate on the "big picture" of a God who, in Dante's words, is "the Love that moves the Sun and the other stars." From love revealed in creation, including our own, we then reflect on our own sinfulness and our need for interior freedom from all that gets in the way of our loving. In our brokenness, we savor love expressed as God's faithfulness and mercy to us, which we often experience through the words and gestures of others.

The main portion of the Exercises is an extended consideration of Divine Love incarnate in the person of Jesus. Contemplating his life, death, and resurrection, we encounter Jesus, who teaches us how to love. Walking with Jesus, we understand better our purpose, our calling in life, and how it fits into God's dream for the world. The crescendo of the Exercises is a soaring contemplation on the love of God. In Ignatius's grand vision, God dwells in all things, and God's love animates all of creation, including our individual lives. Such an awesome gift naturally inspires us to love in return—not just in words, but in deeds. As a school of loving, the Exercises help us come to know more deeply a God who is love, and love by its nature always shares and welcomes others in.

# Paying Attention

One often overlooked expression of loving is paying attention, which is foundational for Ignatian spirituality. If God dwells in all things and all people, then we can appreciate and respond to that divine presence only if we first notice it. The Academy Award–nominated film *Lady Bird* (2017) is the story of an endearing and complicated relationship between a mother and teenage daughter in Sacramento, California. In a pivotal scene, the daughter, who goes by the nickname "Lady Bird," meets with the principal of her Catholic high school, a nun, who reviews her college admissions essay. The principal observes, "You clearly love Sacramento." This surprises Lady Bird, whose distaste for her hometown is evident in the film. The teenager shrugs, "Sure, I guess I pay attention." With a knowing and affectionate look, the nun replies, "Don't you think maybe they are the same thing? Love and attention?"

So much gets in the way of our paying attention. Information overload, multitasking, ubiquitous screens, fixating on the past, and stressing about the future distract us from living with purpose. Even our well-intentioned activity can get in the way of focusing on what and who matters most. In his wonderful book *In the Shelter*, the Irish theologian and poet Pádraig Ó Tuama shares the story of a twelve-year-old girl he met as part of his work in leading retreats for schoolchildren in West Belfast. Relying on Ignatian spirituality, Ó Tuama introduced them to a prayer exercise in which they imagined walking and talking with Jesus. The girl told him: "When [Jesus and I] were talking, it felt nice to be listened to. My mum and dad love me and all, but they are often very busy doing all the things for me, and when I talk to anyone, there's so much noise. So it was nice to be listened to." This story, Ó Tuama explains, demonstrates the difference between "busy love" and "listening love."

In his noteworthy commencement address at Kenyon College in 2005, the author and essayist David Foster Wallace began with a story about *not* paying attention to what is most important:

There are these two young fish swimming along and they happen to meet an older fish swimming the other way, who nods at
them and says "Morning, boys. How's the water?" And the two
young fish swim on for a bit, and then eventually one of them
looks over at the other and goes, "What the hell is water?"

The reason we miss the obvious, Foster explained, is that we are blinded by
what he called our "natural, hardwired default setting" that makes us "see
and interpret everything through this lens of self." Sure, college teaches us
how to think, he observed, but just as important, education (and, I would
add, good religion) teaches us *what* or *who* to think about: people other
than ourselves, interests other than our own.

Such a change of perspective can even transform into something miraculous
a setting with which we are too familiar: waiting in a crowded checkout line at a
grocery store after a long, hard day at work. Wallace told the graduates:

If you've really learned how to think, how to pay attention, then
you will know you have other options. It will actually be within
your power to experience a crowded, hot, slow, consumer-hell-
type situation as not only meaningful, but sacred, on fire with
the same force that lit the stars—compassion, love, the subsur-
face unity of all things.

This all sounds great, Wallace admitted, but to get there, we need to choose
it; we need to actually pay attention. Wallace was channeling Ignatian spirituality (though he probably did not realize it). Pay attention to what's
happening on the inside so that we can free ourselves from dehumanizing
default settings, such as thinking the world revolves around us. Be attentive
to what's happening outside of us so that we can consider realities other
than our own, the miraculous or awesome in our midst. To pay attention is
to reverence ourselves and one another as good and beautiful, even holy.

Such reverence inspires gratitude, a chief virtue for Ignatius, and gratitude opens us up even more to God and others and inspires us to give in

return: to love in deeds not just words. We cannot show gratitude unless we first notice the gift before us: a person, an ordinary meal, a mild and sunny day, a sunset on the horizon, a bowl of chocolate ice cream. Like those fish swimming in water, we live and move in an environment filled with so many gifts waiting to be discovered and meaning ready to be made. All is gift, Ignatius insists. Meaning abounds. But there is no path to gratitude, no way to meaning making, that does not begin with paying attention.

Living with purpose demands that we work through certain creative tensions. We must pay attention both to where we are walking and to the distant horizon: not so focused on our end that we miss out on what is right around us, not so focused on what's around us that we lose sight of the end that keeps us on track. Like those early Jesuits, we are also meant to be contemplatives in action: not so reflective that we become preoccupied with ourselves, not so active that we miss the meaning that comes with taking time to reflect. Finding the right balance from day to day is challenging, so much so that we might be tempted to simply choose one over the other to make our life less complicated.

Too much is at stake for us to settle for such a false choice and to let life pass us by, living without purpose or direction. The French writer and poet Antoine de Saint-Exupéry, author of the classic *The Little Prince*, wrote: "A single event can awaken within us a stranger totally unknown to us. To live is to be slowly born." The water in which we swim is imbued with such truth, beauty, and goodness that we lose much by not noticing it and by avoiding those creative tensions in all their glorious complexity. They are the path to the Love that moves the sun and other stars and impels us to love in return. For one who lives and loves with such purpose, something greater than Ithaka awaits. As the monk, mystic, and activist Thomas Merton shared in his journal, "He who loves is playing on the doorstep of eternity."

# SPIRITUAL EXERCISES

- How would you write your mission statement, your purpose, your "first principle and foundation"?

- Reflect on people who model for you love expressed as attention. To whom or what might you need to pay *more* attention?

- Read the story of Jesus visiting the sisters Martha and Mary (Luke 10:38–42). To whom do you more relate: Martha, who models "busy love," or Mary, who displays "listening love"? Which muscles do you need to exercise more: the contemplative or the active ones?

- Reflect on the past day, even the most ordinary experiences. What experience stands out as most meaningful? Why? Put another way, where did you encounter truth, beauty, or goodness (which is another way of saying, where did you encounter the Divine in your midst)?

# Chapter 2

# LIVING THE QUESTIONS
## The Meaning of Faith and the Benefits of Doubt

As a young Jesuit, I was sent with two other Jesuit scholastics to northeastern India to work for a summer in a hospital for patients with leprosy, or Hansen's disease. The hospital was a compound of buildings that included a rudimentary clinic, dormitories or wards for the patients, a school for the children of patients, a convent, and a residence for elderly people who, though cured of the disease, could not find housing. Because the hospital was in a remote region, we spent a couple of days in the major city of Kolkata (formerly Calcutta) getting orientated. Our host was a nearly eighty-year-old American Jesuit from Baltimore who had been in the region for decades. John was very tall so it was easy to spot him in the crowded and noisy city streets, where it was also easy to get lost. We ducked into a restaurant to enjoy a quick lunch and did some shopping for essentials. My friends and I were all jet-lagged and overwhelmed by the sights and sounds. Sensing this, John took it slow, even allowing for a nap at the nearby Jesuit college. Our bed was draped with mosquito netting, a necessity in the summer.

As dusk settled, we walked around more, and what was less obvious during our daytime excursion became much clearer: the numbers of people who made their home on the streets. I vividly recall passing by a group of teenage boys sleeping in discarded boxes. The human desperation we saw did not seem to end. Frankly, I wanted to run away and fly back home.

In that moment, a year after professing vows as a Jesuit, I felt a profound absence of God that I had never felt before: *How can there be a God who would allow this to happen?* My heart raged in silent anger.

The next day, my question met a response. With my Jesuit companions, I spent time at Mother Teresa's "home for dying" in the Kalighat neighborhood of Kolkata. Located in a large, one-story, concrete, boxlike building, the hospice featured rows of simple but comfortable cots, each one full. The hospice is the place where people on the street are brought to die with dignity or, for some, return to health. On the day we visited, numerous volunteers from Europe were staffing the hospice. I watched as two of them carried an emaciated older man and laid him on a waist-high, concrete block in the back of the dormitory. There, the sisters from the Missionaries of Charity, the religious order that Teresa founded, bathed and cleaned patients. With gentleness yet seriousness of purpose, they poured water over the nearly unconscious man and washed him. They spoke to him in words I did not understand, lavishing him with more tenderness. My gaze shifted to large words painted on the white wall above the concrete bathing station: THIS IS THE BODY OF CHRIST. My heart, once so heavy, lightened.

My question voiced on the city streets was answered not by a well-reasoned theological argument but by the witness of human compassion and community across visible differences. The hospice became like a church, a sanctuary where holiness was revealed in simple human gestures and words. Far from silent, God was speaking but in a way I did not expect. In India that summer, the question of human suffering often returned, and just as often was met with some expression of human goodness or beauty.

At the leprosy hospital, I met a teenager named Sona who was dropped off and abandoned by her family, who could not care for her. The older women in the ward where Sona stayed cared for her, and in turn, she took care of me. During the first weeks of my stay, I did not know what I was doing. My job in the morning was to bring patients from their ward to the dressing room to have their wounds cared for and bandages redressed. Every day, as I wheeled my old, rickety metal wheelchair into Sona's ward, many women jumped up at once. I tried to impose order but could not speak their language (they spoke Hindi or local tribal languages). Sona laughed as she witnessed this comical though very frustrating scene. After a few days of this minor chaos, I walked into the ward, and it was calm. From her bed, Sona directed who would go with me and in what order. She always saved herself for last. Over the summer, Sona and I became friends. Because we did not know each other's spoken language, we usually communicated with gestures and smiles; her smile was broad and her laugh contagious. At the end of my stay, I gave her a purple flower from the hospital gardens, where something was always flowering. She managed to say "thank you" in English. On the day I left, I learned that her leg would likely be amputated because of the disease's progression.

God and I wrestled a lot that summer in India. As a graduate student studying philosophy, I was used to addressing in a methodical way lots of interesting academic questions, but in India, the questions became very personal: *Why, God, do you allow such good people to suffer? How do I make sense of my Christianity living among good and devout Hindus? Why are there so many different religions? What good am I doing pushing wheelchairs all summer when I could be doing something more "useful"?* Such questions rocked me from a faith too easily insulated from human suffering and fortified by my own need to control. They challenged me to live my faith in concrete deeds of charity and to consider what justice demanded in places where so many bodies were broken by poverty and violence. The questions also impelled me to commit to interreligious dialogue and understanding as part of my formation as a Jesuit. Finally, I had to rethink what I thought was "useful" and consider service first from the perspective and needs of those I wanted to help.

In this chapter, I want to explore with you what we mean by "faith" and how questions and doubts are part of our lived experience of faith and are also signs of the restlessness that comes with being human. In the previous chapter, we explored how living with purpose means focusing on our end while also being attentive to our immediate experience and reflecting on that experience to discern its meaning. If we live with such purpose, questions naturally emerge. If we engage them in the right way, and do not run from them, those questions can help us clarify the end we seek, understand the meaning of our present experience, and make sense of the restlessness we encounter along the way.

Some of us still carry the baggage of being taught that to question is to be disloyal or unfaithful. Far from it. To doubt, ask questions, and wrestle with God can be acts of faith. We can take inspiration from the young Eliezer in Elie Wiesel's *Night*, who was captivated by his conversations with the wise teacher, Moishe: "He explained to me, with great emphasis, that every question possessed a power that was lost in the answer . . . Man comes closer to God through the questions he asks Him, he liked to say. Therein lies true dialog."

# Experiencing Transcendence

Often, we talk about faith as if it were a thing, like money in the bank: we either have it or we don't, in greater or lesser amounts, or we reduce faith to a list of propositions demanding our assent. Far from something we "have," faith is something we "do." Before everything else, before our assent or even dissent, faith is our response to God's activity in our lives and thus is grounded in a relationship, or, as Wiesel writes, in an ongoing dialogue with God. Think about how friendships often begin with questions as a conversation starter. They are a concrete expression of interest in another, including God. Asking questions shows how much we want to know and be known by another.

Just as we spend a lifetime getting to know someone we love in the inexhaustible depths of their humanity, we get to know God by wrestling with questions and talking with others about God. This is the work of theology. St. Anselm, eleventh-century theologian and archbishop of Canterbury, defined theology as "faith seeking understanding." One of my theological inspirations is Monika Hellwig, who taught at Georgetown for many years. Paraphrasing Anselm, she wrote, "To believe means to want to understand, and to want to understand means to be asking questions."

Those questions can arise from explicitly religious experiences such as praying, going to church, participating in religious rituals, and reading Scripture. But they can also arise in less explicitly religious moments, such as when we catch our breath before the awesome grandeur of the natural world, when we love another person in a profound way, and when we struggle with the painful reality of human suffering, as I did on the streets of Kolkata. Such experiences—whether they take place in a house of worship, a crowded city, or the cathedral of nature—can stir up something deep within us, something that begs for a response from us. That response, which can take many forms as varied as human experience, is what faith is fundamentally about.

We unnecessarily complicate things when we start judging our response or that of another: "I don't know the right words," "My response will never be enough," "There is no way I can compete with that person's eloquence or intellect," "I'm not holy enough." Recall the "First Principle and Foundation" of the *Spiritual Exercises*: we are created to love God and others. In Ignatius's mission statement for the human person, we usually focus on loving God and others, and skip over those most important words at the beginning: *we are created*. This means that we are not God the creator. We are creatures, and thus limited. This recognition takes the pressure off. We do not need to have everything figured out and to shape the perfect response. We are instead empowered to welcome questions and doubts as our friends, who invite us into an extended conversation about not only who God is but also who we are. To accept these limited experiences is another way of accepting our humanity, which is a very good thing. To run away from our humanity, as we will see later in this book, causes a host of problems.

Because we are beautifully limited beings brushing up against what—or who—is unlimited, we are understandably inquisitive, restless, and even discontented as we try to respond to an experience of transcendence. By transcendence, I refer to an experience of being caught up in something so real and present to us, yet also so much bigger than ourselves and not of our own making. With the transcendent, we rest between knowing and not knowing, seeing and not seeing. We are like Odysseus traveling on the sea toward

Ithaka, his sights on the distant horizon that seems within reach. Yet as he travels toward it, the horizon remains extended, just beyond his grasp.

I have certainly experienced transcendence while in church. Like incense rising to the rafters, I have felt carried away and upward by beautiful ritual and music and the presence of a supportive community around me. I also have experienced transcendence while witnessing the goodness of others, like the volunteers at the hospice in India. More recently, I recall some moments that seemed almost timeless, with family and friends with whom I reconnected after months of separation during the COVID–19 pandemic. In such transcendent moments, words understandably fail, and even the most thoughtful gestures seem inadequate. Perhaps frustrating at first, these experiences and the questions they spawn are gifts in waiting, for they might impel us to find different, more meaningful ways to respond, an effort that can yield enriched friendships, deepened gratitude, and a livelier faith life.

## Encountering Holy Mystery

To encounter the transcendent is to be in touch with mystery: alluring, elusive, holy. Early in my Jesuit life, a kindly Jesuit mentor with a profound intellect introduced me to a rich understanding of mystery. As a Jesuit scholastic preparing for ordination to the priesthood, I studied philosophy and theology at Fordham University. There, I took a tutorial with William Dych, SJ, one of the world's experts on the theology of Karl Rahner, SJ, a German theologian of the past century. Rahner was one of the greatest theological minds of his time, driving so much of the Catholic Church's thinking as it constructively engaged the modern world with all its possibilities and challenges. Bill had studied under Rahner and translated many of his writings into English. Rahner can be challenging to read at first, but in our one-on-one sessions, Bill gave me keys to interpreting the German theologian's often long, winding sentences and novel vocabulary. With Bill's inspiration, Rahner would later resound in my teaching and preaching, and in many places in this book.

For Rahner, humans are beings with an infinite horizon because we are composed not just of matter but also spirit. This explains our experiences of transcendence, our yearning for something beyond what is material, imminent, or close around us. Rahner focuses on our distinctly human quality of questioning as evidence of our being made for transcendence. Our questioning, he writes, moves us to an "infinite horizon . . . which recedes further and further the more answers man can discover." This sounds frustrating: the spiritual goalposts constantly moving. Caught between the finite and infinite, the imminent and transcendent, we may be tempted to stop searching and questioning and instead, as Rahner writes, "take flight to the familiar and the everyday." This may mean settling for easy answers, blindly following what others are doing, or escaping in endless streaming of our favorite entertainment. However tempting, such diversions ignore who we are: creatures who question. Like a current on a river, questioning is our way forward to both the source and the satisfaction of all our yearning and restlessness: God.

Rahner acknowledges that in the modern era, the word *God* may be an obstacle to faith because the word itself has accumulated over the centuries so many layers of meaning, some of which get in the way of believing. For example, some people associate *God* with arguments to justify religious wars and oppression; others find it difficult to get beyond strictly masculine images attached to the word *God*. Addressing these and other obstacles that language presents, Rahner suggests another name for God, more helpful in my view and one that fits well with a faith animated by questions: Holy Mystery.

By "mystery" Rahner does not mean something like a puzzle that is pieced together or a murder mystery solved by a clever detective on TV. Instead, God as Holy Mystery points to an experience more akin to loving another person. Consider someone you love deeply: a parent, friend, or romantic partner. The more you love them, the more you can say that you know them, but also, if you are honest, the more you realize how much more there is to know about them. Your unknowing impels you to spend time with them and get to know them more. This kind of mystery is alluring, not frustrating, and questions are invitations, not obstacles. The Irish poet and theologian John O'Donohue wrote that "a question is really one of the forms in which wonder expresses itself."

Fueled by a deep desire to know, our unknowing or wondering leads us to fall ever more deeply in love with our beloved, whose depths as a person are never reached, thank God—that's why love is so captivating and why we often describe love as transcendent! Faith is an encounter with the God whom we name Holy Mystery (or whatever name you wish to give the Divine), the One who speaks to us from the depths of our being as well as summons us to a remote horizon just beyond our reach. Thinking of faith in this way, our experience of God is a relationship rooted and grounded in love, a lifelong adventure to the heart of God. In the opening of his *Confessions*, written in the late fourth century, St. Augustine distilled for the ages what this adventure is all about: "You have made us for Yourself, O Lord, and our hearts are restless until they rest in You."

## Doing the Work of Theology

Over the course of the semester with Bill, I realized how much I had boxed God into my limited categories. Growing up, I loved the certainty provided by my religious instruction over twelve years of Catholic schooling. I knew where I stood. In this "checklist" approach to faith, I was told what I could do and not do and what calling myself a Catholic required me to profess (even if I didn't always understand what I was saying). As I got older and experienced the more complicated realities of human life, my mind and heart outgrew this approach. All those years of religious formation in my home, school, and parish were invaluable in providing a sturdy foundation to ground me, but as I left for college, I realized how much I needed a more adult relationship with God.

During my first semester in college at Georgetown, I took a theology course called The Problem of God. That title should have indicated that my eighteen-year-old world was about to be rocked. The course was an introduction to theological reasoning. We explored classic questions such as whether we can rationally prove the existence of God, how to reconcile the goodness of God with the reality of human suffering, and how to understand the relationship between science and religion. We studied Christian thinkers and atheist writers: Augustine and Aquinas alongside Sartre and Nietzsche. That semester, I walked around as if I were in an existential haze. For the first time in my life, I was pushed to articulate why I believed what I said I believed. Familiar presumptions were challenged as I talked with people who had different belief systems. I stretched my thinking, and ultimately my praying, in a way I did not expect. My faith deepened profoundly, but it was not always easy. Just as athletic achievement requires challenging physical exertion, so does spiritual progress.

The "problem of God," I now understand, is not that we ask challenging questions but that we think and talk about God in a way that turns God into a curiosity piece or a creation of our own making. Resistant to change, we render faith so comfortable that we are not challenged to grow and put our faith into practice. We domesticate God so that God no longer surprises us. This is a faith that is safe but not life giving or interesting—or capable of growth. With its provocative questions, a thinking faith is one that will last a lifetime because it can handle all the complexities of human living, all the ups and downs. Good theology and a lively faith practice help us encounter the *living* God, to use a recurrent biblical image. The living God is One who matters to me now. The living God might unsettle as much as console.

As the collected wisdom of women and men through the centuries, theology offers different ways to work through our doubts and form questions that are meaningful for contemporary believers. This tradition reminds us that we wrestle with questions in a community of fellow pilgrims, both past and present, each contributing something to "faith seeking understanding." Our dialogue with the Divine never ends, only deepens, and, like friends who have known each other over a lifetime, we may sometimes fall silent before Holy Mystery. Or, as Bill reminded me many times, theology often ends on its knees.

Two weeks after our last tutorial, Bill died. A reticent man, Bill kept private his long struggle with cancer, but the Jesuit grapevine rarely withers, so I knew about his condition. In our last session, we talked about Rahner's eschatology, a field of theology that explores what happens after we die and the world ends. In that last session, Bill was more pensive than usual, but seemingly at peace. Both Bill and Rahner expected, after their deaths, to enter fully into the Mystery who had summoned them their whole lives. This is the eternal home where, to use Elie Wiesel's image, after a life raising questions as prayers to God, "question and answer would become one."

# Asking the Right Kind of Questions

Let me now add some nuance to my urging you to embrace questioning as an act of faith. Here again I rely on Professor Hellwig: "Clearly one must ask questions," she observes, "but they ought to be the right questions asked the right way." Through the learned Moishe, Wiesel concurs, "I pray to the God within me for the strength to ask Him the real questions." Consider questions as just another current on the river we travel as pilgrims. To get where we want to go, we need to navigate the right currents.

What makes a question "right"? The questions that are most helpful are those grounded in a sincere desire to know someone or something better. They help us understand where we are going and what is happening as we travel there. They help us go deeper, leading us to genuine insight, to another life-giving question, or even to a reverent silence pregnant with possibility for something new to emerge. They also serve to create and deepen relationships among those believers and seekers who are also wrestling with questions and answers. The "right" questions help us make sense of our restlessness and live more purposefully.

Other kinds of questions deaden growth or diminish others. They undermine learning by leading to superficial answers. They weaken friendship with God and others. These destructive questions are so laden with suspicion, cynicism, or resentment that no deepening of understanding or relationship can follow. Similarly, questions that are vehicles for self-promotion or proving ourselves right leave little room for something new to be revealed. No God of surprises can emerge there. In our politics we can point to too many examples of questions and inquiry that seek only to divide and take down. Sadly, our faith communities are not immune from such tactics.

Professor Hellwig presents us with another category of questions that she calls "dangerous." These are questions that challenge, provoke, or unsettle us, but in a good way. They push us beyond the known and familiar to a new frontier where we experience God or another person in a novel, refreshing way or grow personally in ways we could not have imagined. For Hellwig, these hard or dangerous questions may reveal that our faith, or more specifically the Gospel, "is really much more demanding than we had previously thought." They direct us to an unexpected but adventurous path. In our complacency, we might be tempted to remain in our comfort zone and avoid such questions, but if we confidently, even courageously, take them on, they can lead us to remarkable places of growth.

My experience in India, and the questions it raised, challenged my understanding of my faith: I became a better Christian the more I appreciated the religious convictions of my Hindu neighbors. I began to see religious diversity as an expression of God's creativity and beauty. As I learned to accept the help of the patients and staff at the hospital who introduced me to their culture, my self-satisfied individualism and materialistic tendencies were challenged. In their place, I found a remarkable new community and freedom from unnecessary attachments that even my vow of poverty had permitted.

I was reminded of these lessons a few years later when I served as a chaplain in immigration detention centers in Los Angeles. Admittedly, I had not previously taken the cause of migrants close to my heart, even though I immigrated from Canada when I was very young (an easier migration than most of today's migrants crossing seas and deserts) and even though the Bible and Catholic social teaching are replete with references to caring for migrants and refugees.

My conversion of heart began as I spent my days listening to the stories of migrants from Mexico, Central America, and East Asia. I prayed with women separated from their families. I walked around the small, enclosed concrete recreation yard with men who shared their life story with me. On my last day, one of them gave me a penciled sketch of the Virgin of Guadalupe, a devotion common among migrants from Mexico and Latin America. Another gifted me with a rose made out of toilet paper, tinted with green and red dye from diluted M&M's from the vending machine. I carry both mementos with me wherever I live, so that I can keep the care and advocacy of migrants central to my identity as a Jesuit and a citizen. Questions have led to greater commitments: working with the Jesuit Refugee Service, writing and preaching about the needs of migrants, promoting first-generation and undocumented students, and spending time on the Arizona-Mexico border and in a refugee camp in Kenya. Questions are "dangerous" in a good way when they wake us up to people we previously overlooked, remind us of our shared humanity, and get us thinking about issues we did not prioritize because they did not affect us directly.

Dangerous questions can also help us identify language and images of God that have become obstacles in our faith development. Because we are dealing with Holy Mystery, no single word, name, or image of God will suffice. Attempts to limit God to one image are usually attempts to control God or use religion for selfish ends. Theologians, for example, have exposed the limits of militaristic, imperial, and gendered language applied to God over the centuries.

Our sincerely voiced questions lighten the path of rediscovering who God is for us, especially when we outgrow images of God and need something more satisfying. As limited creatures we need various images to make present what is transcendent and help us talk about it. Painters and sculptors have unleashed the power of art to bring the Divine closer to us. Compelling artistic portrayals of God can reach beyond our intellect to our hearts, stirred by beauty, and make God present in some way. But those images, even the most beautiful, are not God—just as a photo of your parents is not your parents.

A variety of images of God compete for attention in our heads. Like so many others, in my parish elementary school in the 1970s, I drew actual pictures of God. My artistic renderings yielded a portrait of God as a kind, old man on a heavenly perch, keeping track of when I was naughty and when I was nice. I carried this divine Santa in my head for years, and even now from time to time, the image reemerges. This God is benevolent, though removed from my daily life. The Santa God is appealing because I know exactly where I stand. Do this, and I'm on God's good side and God will leave me alone; do that, and I'm in trouble. In adolescence, my divine Santa morphed into the familiar image of God as a divine accountant, even judge, meting out rewards and punishments.

These images reflect some truth: God does care about what we do, and moral guidelines, based on the wisdom of religious traditions, help us live a meaningful life. Yet God is so much more than that. God wants a relationship with us that is defined not by blind or servile obedience, but by love, even friendship. The writer Anne Lamott, in her typically down-to-earth style, described the God of our childhoods as a "high school principal in a gray suit who never remembered your name but is always leafing unhappily through your files." She recommends lightening up a bit: "If this is your God, maybe you need to blend in the influence of someone who is ever so slightly more amused by you."

The image of God as wanting our friendship has transformed my faith over the years, helping me let go of a one-dimensional, even fear-inducing understanding of God. In high school and college, I came to understand Jesus as the ultimate image of God. This God was accessible *and* cool. My Catholic high school, of course, featured *Godspell* as one of its spring musicals. It depicted a groovy, charismatic Jesus who loved hanging out with his friends. Pictures of the "laughing Jesus" were omnipresent: Jesus in the midst of a good laugh, head rolled back cheerfully, and long, very seventies hair flowing freely. You cannot find a cooler, albeit goofy, representation of Jesus than that! Figuring out the whole human and divine thing remained a challenge, but God revealed in the person of Jesus was easier to relate to. This is a God who listens intently, cares deeply, heals freely, laughs easily, and eats a lot. The Jesus of my youth was more concerned that we live with compassion than follow hard-to-understand doctrines; my younger, very practical self welcomed this shift. Jesus was my friend, a very cool friend.

William Barry, SJ, was an American Jesuit who relied on the image of God's friendship with us as a cornerstone of his theology. This was not some sort of New Wave theology but instead was deeply grounded in tradition. In the *Spiritual Exercises*, St. Ignatius suggests that we imagine having a conversation with Jesus "as one friend speaks to another" (SE 54). Elsewhere, Ignatius advises that we begin a time of prayer by imagining how "God our Lord beholds me" (SE 75). Not scolding, not judging, but beholding, gazing with love, even encouraging. In his autobiography, Ignatius describes a profound experience of God working with him as a schoolteacher works with a pupil. This image, coming later in life, presented him with a God who is there to help us.

The Bible, in both the Jewish and the Christian Scriptures, offers many compelling images of God eager for friendship with us. For example, in the New Testament, the author of John's Gospel opens the book with Jesus meeting his disciples for the first time, in a way similar to how we might get to know someone today. Running across Andrew and an unnamed disciple, Jesus asks, "What are you looking for?" Intrigued by this encounter, they respond not with an answer, but with their own question: "Where are you staying?" Desire meets desire. Jesus responds with an invitation, not an order: "Come, and you will see" (John 1:35–39). Their friendship begins and expands to include others. Fast-forward to the Last Supper, where the Gospel writer sets the scene with some of the sweetest words in the Gospels: "[Jesus] loved his own in the world and he loved them to the end" (John 13:1). Jesus does not let his distinctive authority get in the way of deepening and authentic friendship. At the Last Supper, Jesus tells his disciples, "I no longer call you slaves, because a slave does not know what his master is doing. I have called you friends, because I have told you everything I have heard from my Father" (John 15:15). The Gospel ends with the resurrected Jesus in dialogue with Peter. Three times, Jesus asks Peter a simple but profoundly human question: "Do you love me?" (John 21:15–19), to which Peter, who not too long before denied three times that he even knew Jesus, replies affirmatively and enthusiastically.

These tender images of God as desiring our friendship enrich our understanding of God without exhausting it. God remains God who is transcendent, yet also close to us, as close as friends, loving to the end. God offers friendship and does not demand it. God simply delights in our company. As attractive as this image is, it is still not enough. Better to let a variety of images or names of God be at play in our imagination, each revealing something of the divine mystery that allures us.

# Embracing Our Doubts

Jesuits love asking questions, about anything really, but especially about God. This is one of the reasons I was attracted to them in the first place as an undergraduate. Questions are formed in community. Whether in a chapel or classroom or over coffee or a drink, Jesuits raise questions and suggest answers based on the words and thoughts of wisdom figures and spiritual seekers across the ages. I relish this back-and-forth with an equally inquisitive conversation partner because the best ideas are tested in a lively, thoughtful exchange. All the better when the person has a different perspective than my own. And most important: neither of us is absolutely certain but humbly open.

Pope Francis, a Jesuit at heart, raised a helpful caution: "If a person says that he met God with total certainty and is not touched by a margin of uncertainty, then this is not good. . . . If one has the answers to all the questions—that is the proof that God is not with him. It means that he is a false prophet using religion for himself. The great leaders of the people of God, like Moses, have always left room for doubt. You must leave room for the Lord, not for our certainties; we must be humble." Francis's words are consoling, because I still experience doubts at times. Encountering Holy Mystery, in which we both know and do not know whom we are approaching, doubts naturally arise. The key is not to freak out when they do.

My icon for staying calm in the face of doubt is the beautiful scene in John's Gospel (20:24–29) where the disciple Thomas misses the gathering when the risen Jesus first appears to the disciples, who are sheltering in a locked room. They later share this good news with Thomas. Given that the Resurrection is something entirely new, Thomas understandably doubts that Jesus has risen from the dead and demands that he must see him before he will believe. Jesus responds not by striking Thomas dead with a lightning bolt from heaven, but by showing up a week later and revealing himself, even inviting Thomas to touch the wounds of his crucifixion still exposed on him. Seeing and hearing is enough for Thomas. He responds with the greatest statement of faith in all the Gospels: "My Lord and my God!" a response that was worth the wait.

I imagine the turning point for Thomas was not the dramatic and visceral nature of Jesus' appearance, but that Jesus showed up at all, and when he did, he greeted Thomas calmly, patiently, even lovingly. He loved Thomas as he needed to be loved, giving him time and space to adjust to a whole new reality breaking in. Jesus wanted to be known by Thomas, his friend. Thomas gets a bad rap, for in the end, he's more believing Thomas than doubting Thomas, and he is very much like the rest of us. God can handle our doubts. It is we who need to be more understanding in the face of them.

As varied as the people asking them, questions and doubts emerge from the crucible of human experience, with all its ambiguities. We reflect on our lives, and questions stir; doubts emerge. Some questions find voice in words; others simmer or percolate just below the surface. Regardless of how or whether they are expressed, those questions—even the dangerous or hard ones—are just part of being human. We do not need to feel guilty about asking questions. God can handle it! Rabbi Abraham Joshua Heschel assures us, "We are closer to God when we are asking questions than when we think we have the answers."

Questions that go to the heart of the matter are meant to be lived more than answered definitely, once and for all. We do well, then, to heed the advice of the German poet Rainer Maria Rilke, who counseled a young poet "to have patience with everything unresolved in your heart and to try to love the questions themselves." He offered counsel in words that ring true for us today: "Live the questions now. Perhaps then, someday far in the future, you will gradually, without even noticing it, live your way into the answer."

"Live the questions" can be exceedingly frustrating advice for someone who wants more clarity in a frequently chaotic world or has long wrestled with their faith and desires some peace. As one who yearns for answers too and struggles with impatience, I get it. Yet Rilke's counsel is not an exercise designed to aggravate or test us, but an invitation to greater depth, in a culture that tempts us to superficiality and easy answers. With Rahner, we eventually recognize that, in our encounter with Holy Mystery, every answer is just the beginning of a new question. We learn to appreciate that questions that unfold into other questions are unexpected gifts, as special as a loving relationship that continues to surprise.

If, in the end, we fall silent, or fall to our knees, this is no sign of failure, but the surest indication that we are headed in the right direction, because the end of our pilgrimage, with its paths both winding and straight, is God, whom we call Holy Mystery. If we persist on the journey, with its signposts in the form of questions, we might discover something remarkable: this God whom we seek and question is actually seeking us more.

## SPIRITUAL EXERCISES

- Which questions or doubts do you have that are related to your spiritual journey? They might be explicitly religious questions about who God is or about the practice of your faith tradition. Or they might be questions about challenging human experiences. Which questions are helpful and constructive? Which are not? Which are "dangerous" or particularly challenging for you? Discuss with a trusted friend these questions or doubts. Or simply write them down and pray over them, voicing them to God (however you imagine God).

- Which images or descriptions of God have you relied on? How are they helpful? How are they limited? Which images do you need to let go of? Which images or names for God appeal to you now? For example, Rahner suggests "Holy Mystery." The Irish Jesuit and spiritual writer Brian Grogan, SJ, proposes "Loving Presence." Author and advocate Greg Boyle, SJ refers to "The Tender One."

- In his *Spiritual Exercises*, St. Ignatius suggests that we imagine having a conversation with Jesus "as one friend speaks to another" (SE 54). Pick the setting you want. I often talk with Jesus while walking along the beach (no surprise given my Florida roots). This kind of imaginative exercise makes prayer more real. Speak from the heart. Let go of formulistic ways of praying when they are not helpful. *What's on your mind? How are you feeling? What's going on in your life? What are the questions that you have articulated? What are you looking for now in your life?*

# Chapter 3

# LIVING WITH DEPTH
## Finding God in All Things

I found God on the D train.

Early in my training as a Jesuit, I studied philosophy at Fordham University in the Bronx. The subway—more specifically, the D train—was the quickest and cheapest way to get into Manhattan, about a thirty-minute trip. Having grown up near the beaches and expansive green space of South Florida, I had to get used to the New York City subway system. Admittedly, I was resistant at first. The heat, the noise, and the crowds were less than appealing, until one day, I had an insight that changed my perspective.

On a hot and humid New York day, I was traveling from Manhattan back to the Bronx, unfortunately around rush hour. The platform was packed. The train pulled into the station, and I was herded into the subway car by the pressing mob. It was standing room only. Pressed together like sardines in a moving tin, my fellow travelers and I resigned ourselves to the uncomfortable trek ahead. What remained of the air conditioning was slowly depleted. Even in the limited space, a street performer with an amplifier chose our car to express his very loud artistic talents. Every stop required an awkward dance of people exiting and entering. Tired, hot, and frustrated, I grew increasingly irritable. My typical survival strategy for the subway was to read a book, escaping into my own world, avoiding eye contact and conversation. Given how compressed we were, though, this approach became impossible, so I just looked around, and there I saw it: the kingdom of God.

The kingdom of God, or reign of God, is a central biblical image. It essentially means God's dream for the world, or what the world would look like if God's reign of justice, peace, and love became a reality. If God's reign were realized through our cooperation, we would recognize everyone else as our brother and sister, celebrating their uniqueness while recognizing the bonds that unite us across differences. Of course, this ideal vision cannot be fully realized in our time, given the impact of sin in our world (more on that later). Yet the reign of God breaks into our world at different times. The challenge is to notice this divine in-breaking when it happens.

In the unexpected communion of humanity on the subway, I got a glimpse of God's kingdom. People of different ages, colors, shapes, and sizes brought together for that moment in time. Gazing at the faces around me, I began to imagine the stories each was revealing through the worried creases on their faces and the weariness in their eyes. Over the screeching of the rails below, I heard conversations in different accents and a variety of music beats escaping through earphones around me. In a bygone era—smartphones were not omnipresent—my looking around occasionally met the wandering gaze of another; we connected for an instant, exchanging a silent acknowledgment: "We are in this together."

The subway car was charged with something I had failed to notice on my previous trips, when I was just trying to get through it so I could emerge from New York's underground world to the light above. On that day, the light was below. In a real, almost indescribable way, I felt that I was connected to those strangers and fellow travelers, and I wanted so desperately to know where they came from and where they were going. The subway was the great equalizer. No one cared about how much money someone had or the fancy title on a business card. We were all human beings, brought together for a time, sharing this common project to get from one place to another. We all mattered to one another and to God, creator of us all, our blessedly diverse traveling community.

As the subway car gradually emptied and I was left with only a few others by my journey's end, I experienced some relief, but weirdly, a sense of loss as well. I would not see these people again until, I realized, God gathered us all together in the kingdom beyond the world we know now. For a short time, however, the reign of God broke into my life, in the most unlikely of places, on the D train to the Bronx.

A few years later, I read a reflection by the Trappist monk, mystic, and peace activist Thomas Merton, whose experience of divine in-breaking helped me make sense of that subway ride. One day in March 1958, Merton left the Trappist Abbey of Our Lady of Gethsemani for an appointment in nearby Louisville, Kentucky. On the corner of Fourth and Walnut Streets, he described this epiphany:

> In Louisville, at the corner of Fourth and Walnut, in the center of the shopping district, I was suddenly overwhelmed with the realization that I loved all those people, that they were mine and I theirs, that we could not be alien to one another even though we were total strangers. . . . Then it was as if I suddenly saw the secret beauty of their hearts, the depths of their hearts where neither sin nor desire nor self-knowledge can reach, the core of their reality, the person that each one is in God's eyes. If only they could all see themselves as they really *are*. If only we could see each other that way all the time. There would be no more war, no more hatred, no more cruelty, no more greed . . .

Merton famously summarized this experience, "There is no way of telling people that they are all walking around shining like the sun."

In this chapter, we will explore such experiences of transcendence as moments when we live with greater depth. Recall our previous discussion about faith as a dynamic relationship, an encounter with Holy Mystery in which we live the questions. Asking the right questions in the right way helps us to deepen our learning and enliven our relationship with God and others. This could lead us to think that faith is all our own doing: if I say the right words, ask the perfect question, or do the right thing, then God will appear. This is treating God like a heavenly vending machine that delivers treats only if we insert the right coins and push the right buttons. To the contrary, we do not have to do anything to summon the divine presence: *God is already here.* Whether on a subway or street corner, God waits for us and is always trying to get our attention. And even better, God gives us the desire and ability, even patience, to notice this divine breaking-through. Inspired by our wonder, we learn to see, hear, and feel more deeply so that we can appreciate the divine that is present in the awesome richness of the human experience.

# Living in a World of Grace

In her Pulitzer Prize–winning book *The Color Purple*, Alice Walker offers a captivating image of a generous, even eager, God who is trying to get our attention. Walker derives the name of her book from an insightful dialogue between two central female characters, Shug and Celie, speaking in their dialect about who God is for them:

> Listen, God love everything you love—and a mess of stuff you don't. But more than anything else, God love admiration.
> You saying God vain? I [Celie] ast.
> Naw, she [Shug] say. Not vain, just wanting to share a good thing. I think it pisses God off if you walk by the color purple in a field somewhere and don't notice it.
> What it do when it pissed off? I ast.
> Oh, it make something else. People think pleasing God is all God care about. But any fool living in the world can see it always trying to please us back.
> Yeah? I say.
> Yeah, she say. It always making little surprises and springing them on us when us least expect.
> You mean it want to be loved, just like the bible say.
> Yes, Celie, she say. Everything want to be loved. Us sing and dance, make faces and give flower bouquets, trying to be loved.
> You ever notice that trees do everything to git attention we do, except walk?

God wants to communicate all of who God is with us, which, when you think about it, is just what lovers do: they share themselves with those they love, with the hope that the other responds in a similar way. God's generous love for us and our world hopefully inspires and meets our own love and gratitude. God is not playing hide-and-seek with us or testing us (though we might have an image of God that indicates just that). Instead, as Walker writes, God keeps springing on us little surprises, like a field resplendent in the color purple, until we wake up and notice. God keeps waving at us like trees swaying in the wind. When we do notice, all God wants to say to us is: "Enjoy!" However enticing this invitation, we still may not believe this very good news, thinking that religion needs to be more complicated than that.

In his poem "Hurrahing in Harvest," the nineteenth-century Jesuit poet Gerard Manley Hopkins describes walking outside in late summer, looking at familiar natural surroundings and being amazed at their grandeur, as if seeing them for the first time. He writes in verse:

> These things, these things were here and but the beholder
> Wanting; which two when they once meet,
> The heart rears wings bold and bolder.

God waits for a beholder—God waits for *us*—not because God craves attention but because God wants us to delight in what God gives us. When the beholder's gaze meets God's own, our hearts soar as if on wings made bold.

This heart-soaring, deeply felt movement in us—whether we name it *desire, delight, wonder,* or *love*—is itself a sign of God's animating, life-giving presence. Recall Augustine's insight: our hearts are restless until they rest in God. God, our creator, stirs in us the desire to approach the infinite, to know and be known, to love and be loved. God is *that* close, in the deepest part of every person. That's why all those people around us are walking around, shining like the sun. That's why each of us is brilliant light. Pope Francis embraces this hope-filled view of the human person. Early in his papacy, he said: "I have a dogmatic certainty: God is in every person's life. God is in everyone's life. Even if the life of a person has been a disaster, . . . God is in this person's life."

Most of us can relate to Hopkins's experience of being awestruck by the natural world. Such experiences in nature are moments of transcendence, times when we feel connected with something or someone beyond ourselves that we struggle to name or are content not to name at all. Our heart stirs as the sky bursts into color at sunrise or sunset. We feel wonderfully small as we look up at myriad stars on a cloudless night, an experience of intimate connection that St. Ignatius had in his own life when gazing at the sky and stars. We experience a sense of deep connection with the earth as we listen to waves come onto shore in a rhythm that speaks to our soul. The sound of gentle rain soothes us. The warmth of the sun seeps into our skin.

For some, these are religious experiences. They recognize God as creator of all and thus the giver of these good gifts, to which they respond with a spoken or silent prayer of thanks and praise. Others may not address a prayer directly to God but instead just dwell silently and reverently in the beauty surrounding them, which is just another way of praying, of being in relationship with the Divine. The American novelist and poet Wendell Berry describes such a profoundly spiritual experience in his poem "The Peace of Wild Things":

> When despair for the world grows in me
> and I wake in the night at the least sound
> in fear of what my life and my children's lives may be,
> I go and lie down where the wood drake
> rests in his beauty on the water, and the great heron feeds.
> I come into the peace of wild things
> who do not tax their lives with forethought
> of grief. I come into the presence of still water.
> And I feel above me the day-blind stars
> waiting with their light. For a time
> I rest in the grace of the world, and am free.

*Grace* is a theological term, adopted here by the poet. It simply means a gift from God (whatever name we give God). Grace is a tangible, here-and-now expression of God's love for us, a gift that never exhausts that love. By resting in grace, we immerse ourselves in Holy Mystery, our hearts no longer restless, at least for a time. Hopkins and Berry describe transformative moments in nature, but even their words understandably fall short. Because we are dealing with mystery, no word, formula, or insight fully captures an experience of transcendence. Yet because we are humans who question and search to know more, we try to craft a poem or write a song, we utter a word of thanks and praise, or we just fall silent and rest in the peace of wild things, conscious that we are part of something much greater than ourselves.

In another poem, Hopkins exclaims, "The world is charged with the grandeur of God." I love that word: *charged*. If our senses were augmented and attuned in a certain way, we could see, hear, and feel the trillions of atoms and subatomic particles that are constantly in motion around us and within us. Without microscopes, we do not see this cosmic dance, yet with the eyes of faith or a sensitivity for the transcendent, we can experience the world in a deeper way.

Pierre Teilhard de Chardin was a Jesuit priest, philosopher, and paleontologist whose work in different fields of inquiry spanned the first part of the twentieth century. He approached creation with depth of vision that inspired reverence. For Teilhard, matter mattered, because God created it. What was material was also spiritual, charged with God's grandeur. He writes, "All around us, to right and left, in front and behind, above and below, we have only to go a little beyond the frontier of sensible appearances in order to see the divine welling up and showing through." The Divine Presence is everywhere, and "we live steeped in its burning layers." In Teilhard's view, his vocation as scientist was compatible with his vocation as a Jesuit priest: to examine any part of God's creation was to approach the Divine.

Living in the world as Teilhard describes it sounds very appealing, but he also names the challenge: "The world, this palpable world, which we

were wont to treat with the boredom and disrespect with which we habitu-
ally regard places with no sacred association for us, is in truth a holy place,
and we did not know it." We walk by the color purple, unaware. We settle
for superficiality. Nicholas Carr, in his book *The Shallows: What the Internet
Is Doing to Our Brains*, diagnoses the problem in this way: "Once I was a
scuba diver in the sea of words. Now I zip along the surface like a guy on a
Jet Ski."

Why do we settle for skimming the surface and not dive deep? Various
reasons. We are too busy or distracted. We are overwhelmed by information
and our choices as consumers. We may just be too tired to look and live
deeply. We are lulled—or bored, as Teilhard suggests—by the ordinariness
of it and are thus ungrateful. Or we may be too self-critical, thinking that
we do not deserve the bounty of gifts that awaits us as beholders. We may
believe ourselves unworthy of such intimacy with the Divine, or the love
of another person, who mediates the divine caress. "Earth's crammed with
heaven," as the Victorian poet Elizabeth Barrett Browning put it, and we
miss it or dismiss it.

## Cultivating a Sacramental Imagination

The key to becoming a beholder of the holy, one who does not walk by
the color purple or sit around unaware of hints of heaven around us, is to
develop the imagination. Too often, imagination is equated with fanciful
thinking, a flight from reality. Far from it. To imagine is to experience reality so deeply that we gain a different perspective on it. The imagination
takes what our five bodily senses present to us and amplifies or focuses it
in such a way that a whole new world opens for us: a world of grace, the
holy shimmering everywhere. In his novel *Ulysses*, James Joyce describes
this approach to transcendence: "Any object, intensely regarded, may be a
gate of access to the incorruptible eon of the gods."

The capacity to see the world with such intense regard is what theologians refer to as the sacramental imagination A sacrament is something
tangible, ordinary, sensible, or physical that makes present the holy, divine,

transcendent. For example, religious rituals rely on very ordinary things—water, wine, bread, candles, oil—to convey the sacred. For the person exercising a sacramental imagination, nothing is truly ordinary, in or outside of church. A sacramental imagination unlocks for us the awesome potential in all things.

For many people, sports can be like a religious experience, with their own rituals and communal experiences. Athletes speak of being "in the zone": moments when mind, heart, and body flow as one, movement is effortless, and time seems to stop. The Academy Award–winning film *Chariots of Fire* (1981) is based on the true story of two British runners, Eric Liddell and Harold Abrahams, who each faced obstacles on their way to winning gold medals in the 1924 Olympics. As Abrahams contends with anti-Semitism, Liddell wrestles with reconciling his love for sport with his devout Christian faith. In a central scene, Liddell's sister accuses him of sacrificing his faith in favor of running. Liddell assures her that he will become a missionary to China as he had always planned, but for the time being, he felt called to run: "I believe that God made me for a purpose: for China. But He also made me fast, and when I run, I feel His pleasure." With a sacramental imagination, running and other activities can become transcendent experiences that orient us to God.

My father aspired to be a baseball player, but an early injury sidelined him. He eventually got into sports journalism, first in newspapers and radio, and later television. He had a popular radio show in Montreal before moving our family to South Florida, where he began serving as a manager for Jack Nicklaus, one of the greatest golfers to play the game. Unfortunately, none of my father's three children had natural athletic talent, but my brother, Andy, sister, Cathy, and I tried. We lived across the street from a golf course. After dinner, my mom would send us out with our father to throw the baseball or football or sneak in a couple of holes of golf. Other kids from the neighborhood would often join us. These moments were so frequent and ordinary, but even then, I knew that they were special. I now call them graced. To this day, my favorite time to play golf is in the evening, when the shadows stretch across the fairways and the greens take on a rich color. I feel so much at peace, so connected to the earth, and to my father, who died in 2005 from complications related to Parkinson's disease.

My years growing up were spent visiting countless stadiums and ballparks, cathedrals of sport. We would go to the Orange Bowl in Miami to watch Don Shula's Miami Dolphins. I remember being carried away by the roar and cheering of thousands of fans, feeling exhilarated and so connected to strangers, forming in that place and moment a community. In 2004, when my dad was sick, I had a standing-room-only ticket to a World Series game in Fenway Park, as the Red Sox made their long-awaited run to a championship after an eighty-six-year drought. Andy and I returned to Fenway a few months after our father's death. Grief has its own rhythms. Mourning my father, I did not experience peace for several months, even when I prayed through my grief. At that game, however, things changed. The sun was setting over Boston, the spring air was beautifully warm, and the crowd was spirited. I cannot recall the back-and-forth of the game. As the innings passed, Andy and I talked about the many ballparks our dad brought us to over the years, but never Fenway. In the seventh inning, without thinking, we raised a cup of overpriced cold beer and toasted our father: "Dad would have loved this." At that moment, peace settled deep in my soul, in the most unexpected place: Fenway crammed with heaven.

Although he did not use the term, St. Ignatius encouraged us to cultivate our sacramental imagination. In the closing contemplation of the Spiritual Exercises (SE 235–237), he invites us to find God in all things. Consider, he says, how God dwells in all things, in all people, including ourselves. Imagine how God labors at every moment, not just creating the world once a long time ago but continually creating and sustaining us and all that is around us. In a spirit of gratitude, relish how all good things are gifts from God. This bountiful activity is an expression of divine love, and the natural response to being loved is to love in return. For Ignatius, this is our ultimate calling: to love in return—and love, he writes, "ought to manifest itself in deeds rather than in words" (SE 230). The sacramental imagination, far from a flight of fancy, gets us moving. In this way, we imitate the God who is always laboring, out of love for us, for our good and the good of the world.

# Savoring Our Experience

How can we access the world of grace around us? Sometimes we are just blown away by a moment of transcendence that we cannot *not* notice that something special is happening. We are like Moses encountering the burning bush: "God said: Do not come near! Remove your sandals from your feet, for the place where you stand is holy ground" (Exodus 3:5). Such awareness usually comes in the form of an intuition or gut feeling that something important is going on. Or we are at a loss for words to describe what is happening, a sure sign that we are in touch with transcendence because words necessarily fall short to describe Holy Mystery. In his autobiography, Ignatius recounts sitting by a river and receiving as pure gift a profound awareness into all things, so much so, he said, that if he added up everything he learned during his entire life, nothing could compare to the insight he received on that one occasion.

Moments of such overwhelming transcendence—of a gift given to us so freely, unexpectedly—are as varied as the human experience. For example, we feel completely in awe of nature's beauty, steeped in its burning layers, as Teilhard put it. Or we touch transcendence when we fall in love. Consider, too, the moments when we suddenly get a thought or insight seemingly out of nowhere. Finally, recall experiences when time just seemed to stop. Some people experience this timelessness when listening to music or when sharing a meal with family and friends: good food and wine, lively conversation, laughter coming easily, eternity breaking through. Such moments are gifts from God, not just in what we receive but also in our ability to notice or appreciate them in the first place.

The acclaimed Vietnamese Buddhist monk and peace activist Thích Nhât Hanh suggests practicing mindfulness to become more sensitive to transcendent moments, which in his view can be *any* moment, especially the most ordinary. In his delightful book *The Miracle of Mindfulness*, he offers some down-to-earth advice: when doing the dishes, do the dishes! He explains: "While washing the dishes one should be completely aware of the fact that one is washing the dishes." To wash dishes, or any other seemingly mundane activity, "is a wondrous reality," because we are alive in the present moment. We are not thinking about what's next but focusing on what is given to us now. To be obsessed with the past or the future is like being "tossed around mindlessly like a bottle slapped here and there on the waves." In my experience, mindfulness is easier said than done because distractions come easily for me. If practiced, the discipline of radical attentiveness to the present unveils graced reality in the most mundane circumstances.

Often, we realize transcendent moments only *after* they occur, when we reflect on what happened to us. The Ignatian tradition offers a time-tested, easily applicable tool to develop good habits of attentiveness and reflection: the Examen. This is a method of prayer grounded in the Spiritual Exercises. The heart of the practice is a grateful review of the day, finding God or the divine presence "in all things." I have outlined the Examen in the appendix of this book. My favorite definition of this form of Ignatian prayer was offered by the Jesuit theologian and homilist Walter Burghardt: "a long, loving, look at the real." God is found in what is real, so we look there, at our real life. That look is a loving one: we are not worried about analyzing or categorizing, just enjoying or relishing the experience, resting in grace, as the poet Wendell Berry wrote. And perhaps the biggest challenge, it is a *long* gaze: we take time for this contemplative look at our day so that the holy percolating just beneath our awareness can be revealed. If we see reality only clinically, forensically, and efficiently, we miss out.

While the exact length of this grateful review may vary depending on the circumstances, the central point remains: do not rush, but savor your experience. At the beginning of the *Spiritual Exercises*, Ignatius, drawing from his own frenetic life experience, wisely counsels: "For it is not much knowledge that fills and satisfies the soul, but the intimate understanding and relish of the truth" (SE 2). In other words, savor what happens in your life in such a way that the ordinary becomes extraordinary. Like mindfulness, taking a long, loving look at the real requires discipline because the drive to achieve and be productive is strong in many of us, as it was for Ignatius. But mindfulness is time well spent. We become more open to wonder as we plumb the depths of our reality. Recognizing the gifts given to us every day, we also become more grateful, and grateful people are usually happier people.

## Seeing with Loving Eyes

Burghardt's encouragement to take a long, loving look underscores an important point: finding God in all things is not simply a mental exercise or just a matter of our willing to do it. A sacramental imagination is enlivened or stirred in us because, first, we are loved. It exists in the context of a relationship with God and others, whose love unleashes the capacity of our physical senses. In *The Little Prince*, the childhood classic that every adult should read (again), Antoine de Saint-Exupéry named for the ages how love transforms our ability to see deeply all that is created: "One sees clearly only with the heart. Anything essential is invisible to the eyes." On a magical journey around the planets, the little prince learns this secret from a fox he meets at a moment when he is lonely. The prince asks the fox to play with him, but the fox insists that the boy must first tame him. Confused, the little prince asks what the fox means. "To create ties," the fox responded:

> For me you're only a little boy just like a hundred thousand other little boys. And I have no need of you. And you have no need of me, either. For you I'm only a fox like a hundred thousand other foxes. But if you tame me, we'll need each other. You'll be the only boy in the world for me. I'll be the only fox in the world for you . . .

The fox further explains that taming takes time, that "you become responsible forever for what you've tamed."

So gradually, day by day, their friendship forms, until their sad parting. When the fox tells the boy that he will weep when he leaves, the little prince is again confused, thinking that he has hurt the fox. No, the fox responds. Because of their friendship, the fox receives a wonderful gift. He sees the world differently:

> You see the wheat fields over there? I don't eat bread. For me wheat is of no use whatever. Wheat fields say nothing to me. Which is sad. But you have hair the color of gold. So it will be wonderful, once you've tamed me! The wheat, which is golden, will remind me of you. And I'll love the sound of the wind in the wheat . . .

The reason we can develop a sacramental imagination in the first place is that we have let ourselves be tamed by God. Having been loved so personally, so freely, we can see deeply and differently. We can find God in all things. We can delight and wonder! God made us to live deeply as much as God made us to question, because both capacities lead us to God, to other people, to the natural world, and to the truth of who and whose we are. In the words of Dominican theologian Timothy Radcliffe, "believing is seeing with loving eyes."

Seeing with the heart, everything shimmers brilliantly—if we are open to it. Golden wheat blowing in the wind. Water running over dishes. A sun setting across a ballpark. A field in the color purple. We learn to reverence the natural world as charged with God's grandeur. We also see people transfigured, walking around, shining like the sun. Loving and being loved gifts us with insight, "seeing" deep down in things or people, all of which makes daily life a grand theatre of God's awesome and unbelievable creative activity. With this delighting comes duty: that we treat people with dignity and we reverence God's creation. The fox is right: we become forever responsible for what we have tamed, for what and whom we are tied to.

When we love someone, we can look beyond physical blemishes and character faults and see the person for who they truly are: as worthy of love without having to earn it, as not disqualified from affection according to prevailing cultural norms of who is attractive and who is not. When we love someone, we appreciate their fundamental goodness, even when they mess up, because no one is defined by their biggest mistake. We learn to be open even to people who drive us crazy because, seeing first with the heart and not our judgmental minds, we realize that they, too, shine like the sun and reveal Divine Presence to us.

# Learning to Forgive

A sacramental imagination can also help us love our enemies or those who have hurt us. Admittedly, this is a high bar, at least for me. During my Jesuit formation, when I was teaching at Saint Joseph's University in Philadelphia, I brought a group of college students over to Northern Ireland as part of a theology course I helped teach on violence, forgiveness, and reconciliation. We made the trip a few years after the peace accords were signed in 1998 to bring years of armed conflict in Ireland to an end. In Belfast, we joined a meeting of mothers whose children and other family members were killed in the decades-long conflict between Catholics and Protestants. Across their differences, they found common ground in their shared grief. Modeling forgiveness and reconciliation, they committed to teach younger people how to deal constructively with conflict and not perpetuate violence. In Derry, we met with two men in their seventies—one Catholic, the other Protestant—who had been part of opposing paramilitary groups. Having lost friends in "The Troubles," each spoke honestly of hatreds that they had held on to and were trying to let go of. They could barely look at each other, but fed up with so much senseless violence, they were doing the hard work of peacemaking, which begins with truth telling.

These people in Northern Ireland were learning to see others beyond labels that divide. Instead of seeing someone simply as Catholic or Protestant, Irish or English, they saw a mother who mourned the loss of a son, or an old man struggling with the past and trying to leave something better for the future. They met on the common ground, even holy ground, of shared hopes.

For most of us, forgiveness is hard work because our memory runs strong and our hurts cut deep. Forgiving does not mean forgetting. To the contrary, it is important to name the hurt or injustice, a key step to restoration of relationships (if such reconciliation is possible). Living in truth helps to liberate us from the hold that harm may have on us. While not minimizing our hurt or excusing hurtful behavior, we try to see people in a more radiant light: they are more than their worst act; they remain children of God.

Seeing or relating to another person with greater depth means changing perspective, decentering ourselves. When I was struggling with forgiving someone, a wise Jesuit encouraged me to ask the question: *How does God love that person? What does God see in them that you may not?* The writer Anne Lamott contends that "when you're with an awful person, you're not around a villain, you're with a person who's suffering deeply, starving for love." In his work with formerly incarcerated persons and gang members in Los Angeles, Fr. Greg Boyle, a Jesuit priest and friend, adopts a similar perspective. "There are no monsters, villains, or bad guys," he explains. "There are only folks who carry unspeakable pain." Greg can see so deeply because he loves his "homies," as he calls them. They have tamed one another, claiming the other as their own.

This perspective is refreshing, but at least for me, it is hard to achieve. Holding on to resentments and hurts is strangely comforting because they are familiar, and in holding on to them, I remain at the center of the universe! But I know it is false comfort: as the saying goes, resentment is like taking poison and waiting for the other person to die. A limited perspective also prevents me from seeing where I contributed to the breakdown of relationship.

During one of my annual retreats (Jesuits make a weeklong silent retreat every year), I was struggling with a deep hurt and what I had experienced as betrayal. My spiritual director invited me to pray with the crucifixion of Jesus in Luke's Gospel. In this scene, as he hangs on the cross, some people mock Jesus; others divide up his garments. In the midst of such pain and agony, Jesus says, "Father, forgive them, they know not what they do" (Luke 23:34). I had read these words so many times, but they resonated with me differently in my place of pain. Most people, including myself, do not hurt people maliciously or intend to cause pain. We just do not know what we are doing: we are not self-aware enough; we are unfree; we are not sensitive enough to the experience of another. Jesus' words on the cross soften me, and forgiveness begins to stir in me. I become more understanding of others who have hurt me, I reach out in humility to those I have hurt, and I learn to forgive myself for the hurts I have caused. A sacramental imagination empowers us to adopt Jesus's radical vision from the cross—his seeing from the heart—and embrace forgiveness as a profoundly creative and restorative act.

## Imagining Jesus

Jesus saw deeply because he loved and received love so freely. To teach people about God's reign of justice, peace, and love, Jesus took what was familiar to his audience and recast them in his parables as windows into God's dream for the world: sheep and birds, widows and debtors, merchants and fishermen, vines and mustard seeds, weeds and wheat, a pearl and a lost coin. Even more important is how he saw deeply into people, especially those people usually ignored, ridiculed, or marginalized in his society. He approached and healed sick people whom others avoided; he spent time with tax collectors reviled as Roman collaborators; he spoke with women who were subjects of gossip and derision.

Jesus saw with his heart, and he asked his disciples, past and present, to do the same. To help us know Jesus more personally, Ignatius invites us to exercise our imagination when we pray, placing ourselves in a Gospel scene and imaginatively using all our five senses to make the people, places, words, and actions come alive for us today in powerful ways. For Ignatius, this is how Jesus tames us or forms us to look at the world as he does.

One encounter reveals the source of Jesus' freedom and his expansive and insightful vision. A man with wealth approaches Jesus and wants to follow him. He is devout in following the Jewish law. The author of Mark's Gospel writes, "Jesus, looking at him, loved him and said to him, 'You are lacking in one thing. Go, sell what you have, and give to [the] poor and you will have treasure in heaven; then come, follow me'" (10:21). The man left Jesus in sadness because he was not yet ready to leave everything behind. Jesus' love for the man allowed him to see both his zeal to follow Jesus and his attachment to riches. I have prayed this scene many times, using my imagination, inserting myself in the position of the rich man burdened not by riches, but by other preoccupations. In my prayer, I also imagine that, at some point, the man grew in freedom, gave up his wealth, and joined Jesus on the road—all because Jesus gazed on him with love, not judgment. Jesus tamed him, slowly, unleashing in the rich man a freedom he did not have previously.

We live deeply because we are tamed by love. In his first encyclical, Pope Francis described the transformative power of love to see the world and other people differently:

> Faith is born of an encounter with the living God who calls us and reveals his love, a love which precedes us and upon which we can lean for security and for building our lives. Transformed by this love, we gain fresh vision, new eyes to see; we realize that it contains a great promise of fulfilment, and that a vision of the future opens up before us. Faith, received from God as a super-natural gift, becomes a light for our way, guiding our journey through time.

## Living in Community

A sacramental imagination dissolves artificial barriers among people and between what we describe as the secular and the sacred. With walls down, we are left with a world imbued in Holy Mystery. This way of looking at the world is radically inclusive. No single person or religious community has a monopoly on grace. A sacramental imagination demands that we listen to people who are different from us. It asks us to learn from those of other religious traditions or no faith background, because they have something to teach us about truth, beauty, and goodness.

If we can find God in all things and in all people, then sacredness is not restricted to certain people, times, or places. We can find the sacred anywhere, even in baseball stadiums and subways, in people we love and people we struggle to like. Perhaps we confine the sacred because life is easier that way. If we have to be holy only when we go to our religious services, then we do not have to worry about being good to ourselves, others, or the natural world at other times. Church is church; business or school is another thing. What I do on Friday night does not really matter to my Sunday, churchgoing self. If goodness or worth is reserved only for people I like or admire, then I can easily dismiss those I do not like and avoid the hard but necessary work of justice and reconciliation with those who are hurting. Or if goodness is only for people seemingly holier than I, then I can avoid responsibility for living with integrity and purpose. A sacramental imagination helps us live with greater integrity, the different parts of our lives connected rather than compartmentalized.

After sharing this liberating perspective with students over the years, I know what's coming next. They like the expansiveness of this vision. They love how a sacramental imagination calls us to promote the dignity of all persons and reverence the earth, our common home. They want to live with greater integrity, acting like the same person whether they are at work or play, whether on a Friday night or Sunday morning. They are open to doing the work of reconciliation. But this "finding God in all things" perspective gives them an opening: "Well, if God is found everywhere, at all times and places and in all people, then why do I need to go to church on Sunday? I can just pray in my room or outside in nature. And if God is found in all people, then I can just hang out with my friends as my faith community."

True enough, but not enough. The reason a Muslim goes to the mosque on Friday, or a Jew celebrates the Sabbath on Saturday, or a Christian goes to church on Sunday is not (hopefully) just to check a box on a religious to-do list. Instead, we mark certain times and places as holy or sacred to remind us how holy and sacred *all* time and *all* places are. Religious ritual, when done well, tunes our spiritual antenna so that we can see deeply and truly appreciate how the earth is crammed with heaven and how people are walking around, shining like the sun. Ritual is another way that we are tamed by love, formed in our relationships. With this expansive vision in mind, Michael Himes, a Catholic theologian, offers a refreshing definition of church:

> The church is the community that witnesses to the graced reality of the world. Thus the church is not an isolated realm of grace in a profane or secular world. Rather, the church is the revelation of what is true of the whole world. . . . The church's mission is not to say to the world, "Come and be what we are and then you will be engraced." Rather, the church's mission is to announce to the world, "You are already engraced. Aren't you delighted? Come and celebrate with us."

The image of celebration is helpful here (and sadly, too often not reflected in our religious gatherings). Think about birthday parties. We celebrate birthdays not because our friend or loved one is special on only one day out of the year. We throw a party to remind us about how special they are *all* the time and to give us opportunities to express our love for them, to tie ourselves to them more firmly. Otherwise, being preoccupied or too busy, we might forget or not take the time to express how we feel, which is so important to taming one another, to deepening bonds of friendship with one another. In a similar way, we go to church (or another religious service) to remind us that we walk in a world of grace, to celebrate that gift, and then say, "Thank you." Of course, God does not need to hear our thanks, but *we* need to say it because expressing gratitude lifts us and humanizes us and connects us to the one to whom we give our thanks. Gratitude schools us in humility, a recognition that we need one another.

We are created in and for community. Going to a religious service liberates us from self-isolation and counters the pull of individualism too rampant in our culture. There are Sundays when I really need to go to church: it's been a tough week and I need to be around others who can comfort me and help me feel less alone. Or I need the help of others to put my faith into action, such as taking steps to forgive someone. Even if we do not talk to one another in church, we are standing beside one another, our presence speaking volumes. We lean on ancient words and rituals to give voice or expression to what's going on in our lives. Immersed in those words and rituals, I am reminded that, over the centuries, countless others have walked this path, each contributing to a tradition that lives on in my life today.

Once, when I was in a spiritual rut, I complained to an older and much wiser Jesuit that I was bored going to Mass every day (as Jesuits do) and did not want to go. He replied, "Kevin, sometimes we do not go to Mass for ourselves, but for others. We usually don't see the invisible crosses people carry with them into the church. They might need us there in ways we do not fully understand." We are in this together. As the fox taught the little prince, to love another means that we are forever responsible for one another.

As appealing as it is, finding God in all things is not always easy to do. Living with depth is hard sometimes. As in any walk of life, we can get frustrated or discouraged on our spiritual journey. In such moments, remember to hold on to our rudder, the Ignatian tradition. As we have explored together, this tradition helps us navigate such restless waters calmly, realizing that they are part of our journey as pilgrims, moving us along the way. When disoriented, we live with purpose, refocusing on our end and ultimate mission. When distracted, we try to pay attention, taking a long, loving look at the real. When tempted to react, we instead take time to reflect on our experience to discover its meaning. We live the questions rather than avoid them. We approach Holy Mystery in fascination, not fear. In the face of these temptations to live superficially, we scuba dive, not jet ski. We live with depth, striving to see deeply, feel deeply, think deeply, pray deeply, and above all, love deeply.

Not surprisingly, given my family history, my favorite movie is about baseball: *Field of Dreams* (1989). The Academy Award–nominated film depicts the transformative power of a sacramental imagination in a very

Ignatian way. The actor Kevin Costner plays a farmer, Ray Kinsella, who hears a voice: "If you build it, he will come." Ray ends up building a baseball diamond on his Iowa farm. Emerging from the corn are members of the 1919 Chicago White Sox, disgraced by a cheating scandal. Among other players who eventually arrive is his father, who dreamed of being a baseball player and with whom Ray had a falling out before he died. Many people think Kinsella is crazy because they cannot see what he does. But once others start to see with loving eyes—that is, once they start to believe—they too can see the field of dreams.

In the climactic scene, Kinsella speaks to his father (featured at a young age when he was a baseball player):

Father: Is this heaven?
Ray: It's Iowa.
Father: Iowa?
Ray: Yeah.
Father: I could have sworn it was heaven.
Ray: Is there a heaven?
Father: Oh yeah. It's the place dreams come true.
[Ray looks around at his farmhouse as the sun sets, his wife and daughter playing on the front porch in the distance.]
Ray: Maybe this is heaven.

The film closes with father and son playing catch as a stream of cars winds its way to Ray's field of dreams, his patch of heaven on earth.

It turns out that faith is not as hard as we tend to make it, piling on lots of demands and expectations, distancing us from the Divine. Rather than turning faith—our encounter with Holy Mystery—into an exhausting spiritual Olympiad or obstacle course, we stand still for a moment and let God tame us, love us. We let God find us, instead of us always trying to find God. Then we open our eyes, as if for the first time, and see how close heaven is.

# Spiritual Exercises

- Spend fifteen minutes or so immersed in nature or a crowd, and practice being attentive or mindful. See and hear and feel with loving eyes. Try to really notice and appreciate what is around you. Pay attention to every small detail, the sacred in all things. Or do the dishes or some other ordinary activity and stay focused on what you are doing. What surprises you as you exercise your sacramental imagination? What new thing do you notice? How is your mind or heart moved?

- Review your day using the Ignatian Examen as a guide (see the Appendix). Remember, this exercise is above all about gratitude, so after asking God to guide your memory and imagination, say "thank you" for the gifts of the day, and be very concrete. God is found in what is real and ordinary.

- At this point in your life, consider how you are living with depth or superficiality. Are you scuba diving or jet skiing these days? Where particularly are you called to live more deeply and meaningfully: in a particular relationship? In your work or other vocation? In your faith life?

- If you find that you struggle cultivating your imagination, immerse yourself in good fiction and literature or in the arts (maybe music, film, theater, dance, or painting). Whether we are the artist or the audience, literature, music, and the arts have a way of reaching a different part of us, stirring our hearts, inspiring our imagination.

# Chapter 4

# LIVING IN FREEDOM
## Embracing God's Unconditional Love

The cannonball came crashing through the fortress at Pamplona, hitting Íñigo López de Loyola in the legs. The battle did not go well for the outnumbered Spanish army. The victorious French, chivalrous to the end, set Íñigo's shattered leg and dressed his wounds. Humiliated in battle, he was carried back to his modest family castle at Loyola in the heart of the Basque Country, where he would spend nine months in a painfully slow recovery. On his sickbed, the thirty-year-old Íñigo—known to us by the Latinized name he would later use, Ignatius—had plenty of time to stew in defeat and think about his life. The vanity that drove him to become a soldier in service to the king and to defend the Pamplona citadel against all odds stayed with him. After his leg was reset upon his arrival at home, Íñigo noticed a protrusion of bone, an "unsightly bump," as he described it. Preoccupied with appearance, Íñigo had the bone sawed and excess flesh cut away, a gruesome operation he endured stoically. Although the bump was remedied, Íñigo would suffer a limp for the rest of his life. By his own admission later in life, and writing in the third person, Íñigo acknowledged that he was a man "given to worldly vanities" with an "overpowering desire to gain renown."

Anyone who has endured a long convalescence knows how frustrating and tedious the experience can be. Back in the 1500s, Íñigo could not rely on wireless streaming services to pass the time! Popular in his era were tales of chivalry and knightly exploits, so Íñigo asked his sister-in-law, who was caring for him, for these romance novels. None were to be found in the family castle. Instead, she gave him a popular version of the life of Christ and another book with tales of the saints, not exactly the reading he'd hoped for, but they ended up having an impact beyond his imagining.

As he read the books, different thoughts came to him. In his youthful ambition, he continued to dream about life at the royal court, with all its wealth, privilege, and honors. At the same time, he began to imagine a life of humble service like the lives of the saints he was reading about. According to Ignatius, again writing in the third person, "This succession of such diverse thoughts—of worldly exploits that he desired to accomplish, or those of God that came to his imagination—stayed with him for a long time as he turned them over in his mind." In his ruminations, Íñigo noted a difference in how the thoughts affected him. Thoughts of worldly ambition initially delighted him but soon left him "dry and unhappy." Dreaming of a life like the saints, however, left him feeling "happy and joyful," and these feelings persisted.

With members of the household, Íñigo started to talk about God and became more sensitive to God working in and around him, even gazing at the sky and stars for long periods of time. Something was changing in the former soldier. "The result of all this," Ignatius later wrote of himself, "was that he felt within himself a strong impulse to serve the Lord." Despite his brother's protests, Íñigo decided to leave the family castle to test his newly discovered desires. He hit the road, beginning a journey with many twists and turns, a conversion unfolding slowly and often surprisingly. The journey ultimately led him to Rome. There, with the pope's approval, Ignatius and a small group of like-minded and like-hearted men established a new religious order committed to "helping souls," as he often wrote, and doing any work that serves "the greater glory of God," which became the motto of the Jesuits.

Reflecting on his life, Ignatius preferred to describe himself as a pilgrim, an apt description not simply because he would end up traveling many roads across Europe and even the Holy Land but also because "pilgrimage" characterized his inner journey. Sure, Ignatius benefited from profound insights and sometimes mystical awareness, but he also recognized that letting go of old dreams and embracing bigger ones takes time—it's a lifelong process for most people, including Ignatius. The pilgrim keeps walking, always on the way, albeit with more certain steps as the journey progresses. Others join. Surprises await.

Five hundred years after the Battle of Pamplona, Arturo Sosa, SJ, Ignatius's successor as Superior General of the Society of Jesus, reflected on the meaning of Ignatius's conversion for us today: "In the life of any individual there are many instances that offer us the chance to open up to the transcendent, as happened in the conversion of Ignatius. For him, it all began as he recovered from his wound, but similar experiences can arise in other contexts, [like] being in [pandemic] lockdown, in prison, going travelling, or facing the unknown. There are times in life that shake you up and kick-start this process."

While a run-in with a cannonball is unlikely to happen to any of us today, we are all knocked off our feet in other ways. We get sick, or a loved one does. A romantic relationship or marriage falls apart. We lose a job. Those we trust let us down. Life presents Pamplona moments in many forms. Like Ignatius, who after Pamplona walked with a limp the rest of his life, we carry with us our woundedness and vulnerability, often invisible to others. These painful, life-shattering moments can devastate us, but they also can enlarge us if we approach them the right way. They have something to teach us, and they humanize us. At Pamplona, Sosa explained, "[Ignatius's] petty dreams of fame and fortune were shattered, his fantasies lay in ruins at his feet. But the Lord offered Ignatius new ideals, dreams, and hopes, which led him to set out on paths very different to those that, in his poverty, he had once dreamt of. This can also happen to us. Perhaps life is pushing us, gently or painfully, to abandon little dreams we once had for our lives."

This letting go of little dreams and heavy burdens is the path of freedom. In this chapter, we explore freedom in the Ignatian tradition. For Ignatius, freedom is an interior disposition that, like a good rudder, orientates us in the right direction on our journey. It is a sign that we are living with clear purpose and courageously engaging the questions. Freedom comes from living and loving deeply. Liberated from superficial presumptions and restrictive biases, we see the truth, beauty, and goodness of things as they are. The freer we are, the more authentic we become, which means that what we do flows from the deepest sense of who we are. As Ignatius's story attests, the path of freedom is not an easy one, but if taken, it leads to a future of great promise.

## Growing in Interior Freedom

Freedom is often confused with license, which is the ability to do whatever we want, or living without limits. At first, license may sound appealing, but doing whatever we want usually ends up with us hurting ourselves or others—hardly the way to happiness. I love chocolate ice cream, but I get sick if I eat too much. Or if I take your ice cream cone because I want it, it will hurt our friendship. Authentic freedom accepts certain limits for our own good and the good of others. These limits are derived from collective wisdom passed down through the ages as tradition. Limits may also be based on present-day consensus that justly balances personal fulfillment and the common good. By restricting license, limitations facilitate our flourishing as human beings and as a community.

When I was in graduate school in Cambridge, Massachusetts, writing my thesis, I decided to distract myself by planting a garden in our small backyard. I did the research about what and when to plant. I faithfully watered the soil and was so excited to see the first shoots of green as summer approached. Then one day, as the garden started to take shape, I came out to the backyard and saw the carnage: my garden had been ripped apart by the pesky squirrels or racoons in the neighborhood! I had overlooked a most important lesson in gardening: for a garden to flourish, it needs proper fencing! As with tending gardens, so with human living: to flourish and be truly happy, we need limits and direction. To use the image from *The Little Prince*, we let ourselves be tamed or tied to another because in that loving, mutual commitment, we find joy we cannot otherwise experience alone.

Just as there is a difference between freedom and license, there is a distinction between exterior and interior freedom. In *Man's Search for Meaning*, Viktor Frankl describes his experiences as a prisoner in Nazi concentration camps during World War II. Restricted by barbed wire under the watchful gaze of armed guards and forced into manual labor, the prisoners lacked physical freedom. They were told what to do and when to do it, with the threat of punishment and death hanging over their heads. Frankl's insight was that, although we cannot avoid suffering and may face all sorts of external restraints, we are still free to choose how to respond to our suffering and find meaning in it: "We who lived in concentration camps can remember the men who walked through the huts comforting others, giving away their last piece of bread. They may have been few in number, but they offer sufficient proof that everything can be taken from a man but one thing: the last of the human freedoms—to choose one's attitude in any given set of circumstances, to choose one's own way."

In one particularly compelling passage, Frankl recalls trudging along an icy, slushy road with other prisoners on a cold morning, just as dawn was breaking. Prompted by the comment of another prisoner, he started to think about his wife, who, unknown to him, had died in another concentration camp: "My mind clung to my wife's image, imagining it with an uncanny acuteness. I heard her answering me, saw her smile, her frank and encouraging look. Real or not, her look was then more luminous than the sun which was beginning to rise." He continued:

> A thought transfixed me: for the first time in my life I saw the truth as it is set into song by so many poets, proclaimed as the final wisdom by so many thinkers. The truth—that love is the ultimate and the highest goal to which man can aspire. Then I grasped the meaning of the greatest secret that human poetry and human thought and belief have to impart: *The salvation of man is through love and in love.* I understood how a man who has nothing left in this world still may know bliss, be it only for a brief moment, in the contemplation of his beloved. In a position

of utter desolation, when man cannot express himself in positive action, when his only achievement may consist in enduring
his sufferings in the right way—an honorable way—in such a
position man can, through loving contemplation of the image he
carries of his beloved, achieve fulfillment.

This interior freedom is rooted and grounded in a love that knows no limits
and allows the human spirit to soar beyond any physical limitation.

One of the central purposes of the Spiritual Exercises is to help a person
grow in interior freedom. Ignatius experienced that grace on his sickbed, as
the small-minded dreams of his earlier life gave way to a more expansive
and life-giving vision. Frankl experienced interior freedom as love for his
wife liberated him, at least for a moment, from the drudgery and terror of
the concentration camp.

The stories of Ignatius and Frankl are dramatic and extraordinary, but
they are also very human: each of us in our own way, in the circumstances
of our particular life and the various limits we face, is called to greater freedom. We carry around different kinds of internal baggage, which weigh us
down and prevent us from being happy and living a fulfilled life. Ignatius
referred to these weights on the soul as disordered affections or attachments
(SE 1). When we cling too much to what or whom we love, our affections
or attachments become disordered. When our natural desires and attractions become excessive, skewed, or misdirected, they become disordered.
With the tools of Ignatian spirituality, we can become free of disordered
attachments or internal chaos so that we can be free to embrace our fundamental mission: to love God, others, and ourselves. This is the turning, or
conversion, we seek.

# Understanding Sin

For Ignatius, his unfreedoms—his vanity and excessive preoccupation with
himself—were sinful. Sin, like faith, is a theological category. We tend to
reduce sin to breaking a rule or not following a command, but above all, a

sin is a violation of a relationship, which those rules and laws protect and nurture, like fencing around a garden. Sin interferes with our flourishing as human beings and disrupts our relationship with God, others, and the natural world. The Spiritual Exercises deepen our understanding of sin as an offense against God and others, so it is worthwhile here to spend some time reflecting on what we mean by *sin*.

Before doing so, let me emphasize two points. First, our baggage, our unfreedoms, are not all sinful. For example, the despair that Frankl describes is not sinful; rather, it is an understandable reaction to life in a concentration camp. Or the self-doubts that most of us experience are part of being human, and usually not sinful. Still, when indulged, despair and self-doubt can become disordered and get in the way of our flourishing.

Second, talking about sin may not initially resonate with people unaligned with a religious tradition, which is true of an increasing number of people in younger generations who may understand their unfreedoms in categories other than sin. Whether we consider an unfreedom a sin, an impediment to our human development, or a disorder of the spirit, the first step on the road to greater freedom is to courageously but gently deal with our interior baggage.

My favorite definition of sin comes from the Jesuit theologian James Keenan: sin is the failure to bother to love. Central to the Jewish and Christian tradition is the commandment to love God and neighbor, and, we would add today, love the natural world. Sin is love's opposite. If love unites, then sin divides. If love uplifts, sin deflates. If love binds people together, sin ruptures relationships. If love upholds human dignity, sin violates it. If love cherishes creation, sin degrades it.

As a devout Jew, Jesus naturally talked about sin, but he never gave a lecture-like definition of sin. Instead, characteristic of his very personal style, Jesus often told parables, which are down-to-earth, relatable stories that teach a moral lesson through a surprising twist or dramatic turn. His audience is invited to make connections with characters in his stories. For example, Jesus denounces a rich man who ignores the poor beggar Lazarus, sitting outside his home, as he makes his way to a sumptuous feast inside

(Luke 16:19–31). In the parable of the Good Samaritan, Jesus indicts two religious officials who walk by a man beaten up and left for dead on the side of the road, and he praises the Samaritan (traditional adversaries of the Jewish people), who shows mercy and cares for the injured man (Luke 10:29–37). In the parable of the Last Judgment, Jesus condemns those who do not feed the hungry, give drink to the thirsty, offer hospitality to the stranger, clothe the naked, and visit the imprisoned (Matthew 25:31–46). In all these parables, Jesus depicts sin as failing to do something—more specifically, as failing to show mercy or care for another human being in need. Mercy is a sign of living in freedom.

In addition to teaching about sin through stories, Jesus shows through his actions how to treat those who sin or mess up. He hangs out, for example, with tax collectors, who were considered by society at the time to be sinners because they collaborated with the occupying Roman authorities and had a reputation for defrauding people (Mark 2:15–17; Luke 15:1–7; Matthew 9:9-13). In one amusing scene, Zacchaeus, a wealthy tax collector, climbs a tree to see Jesus, who notices the curious man and invites himself over to Zacchaeus's house for a meal. The crowd disapproves resoundingly, but Jesus does not care. The impact of Jesus' bold gesture is a dramatic change of heart in the tax collector (Luke 19:1–10). Again challenging cultural expectations, Jesus encounters a Samaritan woman at a well and engages in a lengthy conversation with her, despite the unfavorable reputation she had among her townspeople (John 4:4–42). In another encounter, Jesus saves a woman caught in adultery and about to be stoned. He condemns the hypocrisy of her accusers but shows mercy toward her (John 8:2–11).

Jesus is a free man. He risks his own well-being or reputation as he challenges herd mentalities and subverts social conventions. For Jesus, the sinner is more important than the sin. The impact of Jesus' mercy is to liberate people to serve others and to find peace or wholeness. Inspired by her conversation with Jesus and the kindness he showed her, the woman at the well brings others to Jesus. The tax collector Zacchaeus gives away half his possessions and promises restitution to those he cheated.

In another encounter that reveals how mercy enkindles freedom in another (Luke 7:36–50), Jesus is invited by a Pharisee, a member of the religious elite, to dine with him. A "sinful woman in the city" crashes the party: "Bringing an alabaster flask of ointment, she stood behind [Jesus] at his feet weeping and began to bathe his feet with her tears. Then she wiped them with her hair, kissed them, and anointed them with the ointment." The Pharisee is appalled that Jesus would let such a woman get so close. In typical fashion, Jesus calls out the Pharisee's condescension and highlights how the woman's hospitality, so important in Jesus' culture, far exceeds that of his host. Speaking to the woman directly, Jesus recognizes her generous expression of faith and wishes her peace. Speaking to the Pharisee, and to us, he teaches an important lesson: "So I tell you, her many sins have been forgiven; hence, she has shown great love. But the one to whom little is forgiven, loves little." The woman did not have to earn forgiveness by her gesture of anointing. Instead, the anointing, so intimate and effusive, was a sign of gratitude for the loving mercy she had received somewhere along the way. Gratitude is a fitting response to being set free.

# Revisiting the Parable of the Prodigal Son

Jesus' most famous story about sin and mercy is the parable of the prodigal son (Luke 15:11–32). He tells this parable in response to the muttering accusation of Pharisees: "This man welcomes sinners and eats with them" (Luke 15:2). As we have seen, Jesus wears that accusation as a badge of honor. According to the parable, a wealthy man has two sons. The younger son demands that his father give him his inheritance, an offensive request that in Jesus' time was the equivalent of wishing his father were dead. The father obliges, and the younger son goes off "to a distant country," where he squanders all his inheritance on a life of debauchery. When a famine strikes the country, and he finds himself with nothing to eat, the younger son, "coming to his senses," decides to go home:

So he got up and went back to his father. While he was still a long way off, his father caught sight of him, and was filled with compassion. He ran to his son, embraced him and kissed him. His son said to him, "Father, I have sinned against heaven and against you; I no longer deserve to be called your son." But his father ordered his servants, "Quickly bring the finest robe and put it on him; put a ring on his finger and sandals on his feet. Take the fattened calf and slaughter it. Then let us celebrate with a feast, because this son of mine was dead, and has come to life again; he was lost, and has been found." Then the celebration began.

We pause here to reflect on the parable's lessons about freedom. First, this part of the parable ends in a great feast. Jesus loves a party: elsewhere he compares heaven to a banquet (Matthew 8:11; 22:2), and his first miracle was to keep a party going at the wedding feast of Cana, where the host had run out of wine (John 2:1–11)! It's not surprising, then, that in the parable of the prodigal son, festivity is a sign of freedom. The father had every good reason to hold a grudge for the son's insult about taking the inheritance, and then his carelessness in squandering his own estate. But like Jesus, the father focuses on the sinner, not the sin. The father is not interested in the lurid details of what his son did in that distant country; he is just happy his lost son has come home, not only physically but also in his change of heart.

For his part, the younger son's freedom is growing, but it's not as complete as his father's. The son, after all, decided to come home only after he was dying of hunger. We assume his apology is sincere, and we can imagine how the father's extravagant (even prodigal) gesture of mercy prodded him along the road to even greater freedom. Growing in freedom takes time. It comes with age and experience, and also with the inspiration of truly free people in our lives, with whom we are wise to surround ourselves.

With the celebration underway, the parable takes a provocative turn. We now get to know the older brother who was out in the field when his brother came home and who now hears the sound of music and dancing as he approaches the house. A servant tells him the news of his brother's return. The elder brother is not happy:

> He became angry, and when he refused to enter the house, his father came out and pleaded with him. He said to his father in reply, "Look, all these years I served you and not once did I disobey your orders; yet you never gave me even a young goat to feast on with my friends. But when your son returns who swallowed up your property with prostitutes, for him you slaughter the fattened calf." He said to him, "My son, you are here with me always; everything I have is yours. But now we must celebrate and rejoice, because your brother was dead and has come to life again; he was lost and has been found."

Again, we witness the father's freedom. For the elder son, love is a zero-sum game: the more love his brother gets, the less love there is for him. For the father, love always multiplies and overflows, never running out. The father loves the elder son too, and freely and honestly expresses that affection. He is trying to love his son to greater freedom. The father's freedom also leads him to name a truth without hesitation, not succumbing to the elder brother's guilt trip: now is the time to celebrate the younger brother's homecoming. In light of the father's freedom, we see so clearly the elder brother's unfreedom, his fuming with jealousy, his refusing to join the celebration. He won't be tamed by love. While the younger brother "comes to his senses," the elder does not. The parable leaves us hanging: we do not know whether the elder son ever decides to join the party. Generations of the parable's audiences have been left wondering what they would do in such a moment.

The parable hits close to home. I have heard and read the parable of the prodigal son countless times and have usually found myself identifying more with the older brother. In my family, I assumed the role of the "good son," always doing the right thing, rarely getting into ordinary, youthful trouble. I, too, would silently fume when my siblings or others were on the receiving end of some authority figure's mercy. That self-righteousness still rears its ugly head at times, when I too easily compare myself to others and get upset when others receive what I consider an undeserved break or when I do not get the reward I think I deserve.

The image of the elder brother stewing outside still challenges and saddens me. It goes to the heart of the matter. So many sins can be reduced to excessive self-preoccupation. Of course, it's perfectly fine to take care of our own needs, which is a proper exercise of self-love, but not when it's to the exclusion of others' needs. Both brothers were self-centered, but in different ways. The younger brother acted with license, not interior freedom. He wanted his inheritance so he could spend it on what he wanted, without regard to his father's feelings, and ultimately not knowing what was for his own good (his spending spree left him dying of hunger).

For his part, the elder brother's self-centeredness meant he did not share in his father's joy. In jealousy, he wanted revenge; he wanted his brother to pay for his betrayal of abandoning not just his father but him as well. He stayed around, but his brother didn't. He deserves the attention, not his brother. Resentment prevented him from embracing the father's larger vision in which worldly justice is enlarged by love, which makes room for everyone.

Mercy invites the younger brother (and us) into the feast; sin leaves the elder brother (and us) isolated and alone. This image of self-imposed isolation resonates with the depiction of Satan in Dante's *Inferno*. There, Dante describes Satan in hell, half-frozen in ice made of his own tears. As Satan beats his wings in a vain attempt to free himself, he creates a chill that keeps the ice encasing him continually frozen. Similarly, for Martin Luther, sin is "humans turned in upon themselves." Richard Rohr, the prolific Franciscan theologian, wisely observed: "I am sure you know that most people do not see things as they *are*, they see things as *they* are!" The freedom we are called to is a change in perspective, looking up, seeing deeply, considering the world beyond ourselves, leaving behind patterns of thought and behavior that trap us in ice, all alone. We are tired of living in distant countries of our own making. Freedom calls us home.

# Discerning Our Unfreedoms

Within religious traditions, we are trained to name sins. I yelled in anger at my spouse. I lied to get out of an obligation. I talked uncharitably behind someone's back. I kept something that did not belong to me. I littered on a highway. Taking this kind of moral inventory is helpful as we try to become better people and mend broken relationships. Naming sins helps us better understand the "fencing" around our lives, which allows us to flourish. However, naming sins risks our skipping over what we did *not* do, or how we failed to "bother to love." These are the "could haves" of our lives that we seldom account for: I could have spoken up to defend someone, but I didn't. I could have taken some time to call a friend in need. I could have taken public transportation instead of driving. I could have spent time serving those who are hungry instead of streaming my favorite show.

A moral or good life requires that we ask not only *what* we did or did not do but also *who* we are becoming as persons. We focus not just on our conduct but also on our character, because what we do flows from who we are. A generous person, for example, does generous things. I lived in a university residence hall for several years. I recall a student who stopped by full of regret for something he had done over the weekend. In the *Spiritual Exercises*, Ignatius points out that sin breeds confusion (SE 48). This young student was confused, frustrated. "That's not who I am," he told me, exasperated, which is exactly the point: his regrettable actions did not reflect who he was, and he and I knew that. With keen pastoral insight, the theologian James Alison suggests that most of us are "human creatures who, basically good, find ourselves inextricably caught up in an addiction to being less than ourselves." The young man wanted to become more like himself, more focused on the needs of others, less concerned about what others thought of him. He was a good person who sometimes, like the rest of us, did wrong things. Most importantly, he was striving to be a better person, a work in progress, a pilgrim on the way.

Ignatius presents an expansive view of sin. Before looking at personal sin, Ignatius asks us to consider the cosmic scope of sin, which he calls the "sin of the angels" (SE 50). Then we pray over the "sin of Adam and Eve" and its impact on humanity (SE 51), which today we might call original sin, or the sinful dispositions that all of us deal with simply by being human. Looking at the bigger picture of sin, we heed the advice of the Irish poet and theologian Pádraig Ó Tuama: "If we are to tell the story of sin, we must tell the story of the sin we live in, not just the sins we commit." We begin to understand how we are caught up in long-standing sinful social structures, such as systemic poverty and racism.

Having immersed ourselves in the cosmic and social story of sin, we who make the Exercises then narrow our focus to our particular sins. We come to understand how the battle between good and evil is waged in the human heart and revealed in our concrete choices. We do not just name sins; we try to understand fundamental weaknesses, inclinations, or sins that give rise to other sins. For example, Ignatius names ingratitude as a chief sin. While gratitude naturally turns us outward to God and others, ingratitude traps us in the tiring drama of our own self-pity or self-involvement, and it causes us to act in ways that do not reflect who we truly are or want to be. Ingratitude prevents us from seeing deeply, from appreciating the Divine Presence in all things and all people. Our world becomes smaller, darker, less wonder filled.

Fear is another interior reaction that can lead to sin or unfreedom. While we want always to avoid ingratitude, we need to discern carefully when dealing with fear, because sometimes fear is the right response. The fear response is designed to keep us out of danger, and it's a natural reaction. As a reminder of just how commonplace fear is, some version of "do not be afraid" occurs 365 times in the Bible; in the Gospels, more than ninety times Jesus urges us not to fear. Fear can protect us. If I am caught in a natural disaster such as fire or flood, the adrenaline that fear produces can save my life. If I have been hurt in a relationship, fear of getting hurt again is a reasonable response, at least initially.

In my experience, however, most fear gets in the way of my becoming the person God calls me to be. It hinders our journey as pilgrims, our growth in faith, hope, and love. It undermines our relationship with others. This limiting fear takes many forms. If I fear getting hurt so much that I never risk committing to another person, then I will miss out on the beauty of loving and being loved in a profound way. If I am too afraid of what others think of me or of being alone, and thus go along with the crowd and compromise my values, then I diminish myself. If I never fully commit for fear of missing out on someone or something better, then I never live with depth. Finally, if my faith is riddled with fear about what God will do to me when I mess up, then my faith stagnates, as does any relationship governed by fear of punishment or disapproval.

Amanda Gorman is an American poet who offered the inaugural poem at the presidential inauguration ceremony in 2021. A year later, in an op-ed in the *New York Times*, she reflected on her own fears and the fears we hold in common. Fear, she writes, "can be love trying its best in the dark." She offers sound advice for us as we discern our fears: "Do not fear your fear. Own it. Free it. This isn't a liberation that I or anyone can give you—it's a power you must look for, learn, love, lead and locate for yourself."

## Accepting Our Fundamental Goodness

The best antidote to fear is love. A simple example: I was scared of the dark as a child. A night light helped, but nothing was better than the hug of my mother, who assured me that there was no need to be afraid. When I was older, when I faced disappointment in my life, her repeated assurance to me—"all will be well"—always soothed me. Anyone who has been hurt in a relationship knows the transformational power of finding love—or being loved—again. We feel lighter, the world looks different, because love casts out all fear. As the Christian Scriptures proclaim, "there is no fear in love" (1 John 4:18).

This is such good news, but it may be hard to believe because we live in a world where love often carries conditions. We receive various messages—spoken and unspoken—that we need to earn love by looking or acting a certain way, achieving a certain status, making a certain amount of money, or hanging out with the right people. With so many conditions, we become suspicious when love is offered to us or we grow anxious that we will not find love. The Dominican theologian Timothy Radcliffe put it this way: "Most sin is pretending to be someone else, admirable or powerful or sexy, who will have value in other people's eyes and one's own. As with the prodigal son, it is a form of self-exile, taking refuge in an imaginary self. . . . Why do we all do this? It is because we fear that without some impressive mask we will not be loved."

For the theologian Michael Himes, the foundational sin is not disobedience or breaking a rule but denying our fundamental goodness: that we are loved just as we are. He bases his argument on the biblical narratives of creation, which stem from two sources. According to the first account of creation, after creating the natural world, God fashioned human beings in God's image and likeness, and then "God looked at everything he had made, and found it very good" (Genesis 1:26–31). In the second story of creation, which describes the origin of sin, the serpent successfully tempts Adam and Eve to eat from the tree of the knowledge of good and evil, which God prohibited them from doing (Genesis 2:16–17). The serpent insists, "God knows well that when you eat of it your eyes will be opened and you will be like gods, who know good and evil" (Genesis 3:5).

According to Himes, what drove Adam and Eve to disobey God's command was thinking that they needed to be like gods to be loved. They forgot that as humans they were just fine: fundamentally good and made in the divine image. In becoming human in the person of Jesus Christ, God reaffirms the original judgment of our goodness as human beings. According to Himes, "Salvation is not the story of God's rescuing us from an evil universe but of God's coming to live in the universe with us so that we finally recognize how good the universe is." When we fail to acknowledge the goodness of creation, including ourselves, sin and pain follow because we are more likely to disrespect, diminish, or discard who or what we deem to be unworthy of love, including ourselves.

God's unconditional and faithful love for us, often mediated through the love of people in our lives, is the dynamite that frees our "rubbled-over heart," to use an image from Jesuit theologian Karl Rahner. Being loved enables us to love more freely and to see more deeply. In the spaciousness of another's love, fear and self-preoccupation find little room to nest. We confidently embrace our restlessness and courageously live the questions, even the difficult ones.

That we sin or mess up does not take away God's love for us: God's love is not conditional. At the beginning of the Exercises, we ask for the grace to accept ourselves as loved sinners. When asked in an interview how he would describe himself, Pope Francis, who as a Jesuit knew the Exercises well, replied by referring to a favorite painting that hangs in a church in Rome, Caravaggio's *The Calling of St. Matthew*. In the masterpiece, Jesus points to the tax collector across the room, as if summoning him to get up. Pope Francis focuses on Caravaggio's depiction of Matthew's response: "It is the gesture of Matthew that strikes me: he holds on to his money as if to say, 'No, not me! No, this money is mine.' Here, this is me, a sinner on whom the Lord has turned his gaze."

Being a loved sinner sounds like a contradiction: if I am a sinner, how can I be loved? This is a question that, in the parable of the prodigal son, the humbled, probably embarrassed younger son would have had as his father ran out to welcome him and celebrated his homecoming with such extravagance. In a worldly calculus of prizing the perfect, the homecoming party does not make much sense. While there is nothing wrong with achievement and success, when we fix too much of our identity on what we accomplish rather than on who we are as persons, we get into trouble. We beat ourselves up. We become resentful of others. We withdraw and despair. We become timid in offering our gifts for the good of others. We become unfree.

To accept our limits does not mean settling for mediocrity. Rather, by dealing with the reality that we are not God and that failure is part of being human, we learn to chart healthy pathways to growth and deal with setbacks more productively and peacefully. We also learn to forgive ourselves. I have always found the words of Fay Vincent, a former commissioner of Major League Baseball, encouraging as I face my own temptation to perfectionism:

Baseball teaches us, or has taught most of us, how to deal with failure. We learn at a very young age that failure is the norm in baseball and, precisely because we have failed, we hold in high regard those who fail less often—those who hit safely in one out of three chances and become star players. I also find it fascinating that baseball, alone in sport, considers errors to be part of the game, part of its rigorous truth.

Acknowledging our own vulnerability can also be a gift because failure makes us more compassionate toward others and more understanding of their shortcomings. Accepting the rigorous truth that errors are a part of life, we learn to be gentler with ourselves and others, and find good company in the human race of beautifully limited people. The Trappist monk, mystic, and peace activist Thomas Merton wrote a brief prayer in his journal that so plainly captures what it means to be a sinner loved by God, here referring to Jesus as the Good Shepherd, one of the names given to him in the Gospels:

> Good Shepherd, You have a wild and crazy sheep in love with thorns and brambles. But please don't get tired of looking for me! I know You won't. For You have found me. All I have to do is stay found.

## Cultivating Courage

Another virtue that helps us grow in freedom is courage. Instead of indulging fear that is destructive or diminishing, we prudently move forward in the face of fear. Amanda Gorman writes, "I look at fear not as cowardice, but as a call forward, a summons to fight for what we hold dear."

We keep walking when we feel like hiding. After a cannonball moment in life, we get up and dare to embrace a larger, different dream for ourselves. We risk loving again. We stand up for ourselves when others do not. We fight for what we believe in. Practicing courage, we develop resilience, and with that, hope stirs in us.

Living in truth—or "coming to our senses," as the parable describes the prodigal son—is empowering and healthy, but naming the truth takes courage. The American Buddhist nun Pema Chödrön wisely observed, "Fear is a natural reaction to moving closer to the truth." This reminds me of my years of ministry on college campuses, walking with many students as they embraced their identity as gay, lesbian, or transgender. Courageously facing their fears of rejection and temptations to self-hatred, they named their truth and claimed it. In so doing, they experienced a deep inner peace and confidence. Many of these students struggled with reconciling their faith and sexual or gender identity, not unexpected given how some religious communities have marginalized and hurt them.

I recall one student coming to my office after months of wrestling with his faith and smiling so broadly, sharing the profound realization, the good news, that God created him in love and loves him for who he is and for how God made him. This was confirmed in the moment that he shared with his family that he is gay. His broad smile was a sign of great interior freedom, which allowed him to love himself and others from the deepest part of who he is. In speaking with him, and hearing his experience, I felt like I was on holy ground. This memorable conversation, and others like it, brought new meaning to a quotation in Latin etched on the wall at the entrance of the university library where the student regularly studied: "You will know the truth, and the truth will set you free" (John 8:32). The truth liberates.

I have also witnessed the transformative power of love and truth while walking with people in Alcoholics Anonymous and related communities. For generations, AA has saved lives and restored families. Those in AA are among the most courageous people I know. Central to AA is speaking and claiming the hard truth, expressed in what is called the first step (of twelve): "We admitted we were powerless over alcohol—that our lives had become unmanageable." Addicts courageously address painful realities about how they have hurt others, but they also come to appreciate the consoling truth that "a Power greater than ourselves could restore us to sanity." Working through the steps with a sponsor and attending regular meetings with other addicts and allies create a remarkable community of loving support that sustains a person in sobriety and witnesses the power of vulnerability and radical honesty.

## Practicing Spiritual Freedom

Every day, each of us can practice spiritual freedom. Naming our sins, limitations, fears, or disordered attachments is a helpful spiritual exercise, the first step on the path to freedom. The truth does set us free, but the path to it is not always easy. We expose the lies that seduce us so that we can be free of them. It is fitting that the author of John's Gospel calls the devil the "father of lies" (John 8:44).

In his commencement address at Kenyon College in 2005, novelist David Foster Wallace called the graduates (and us) to examine our "default settings" that lead us to try to find meaning in things that do not really last. "In the day-to-day trenches of adult life," he said, "there is actually no such thing as atheism. There is no such thing as not worshipping. Everybody worships. The only choice we get is *what* to worship." He invites us to live more consciously and attentively so that we do not end up worshiping the wrong things, like wealth, power, and physical appearance. "And an outstanding reason for choosing some type of god or spiritual-type thing to worship . . . is that pretty much anything else you worship will eat you alive." Instead of license (doing whatever we want), Wallace urges us to embrace freedom that begins with self-awareness, includes discipline and effort, and ends with "being able truly to care about other people and to sacrifice for them, over and over, in myriad petty little unsexy ways, every day. That is real freedom."

Such freedom sometimes means letting go of good things or people we love. As a young adult, I loved teaching high school, yet I discerned that God was calling me to go deeper in my vocation. I left a community and work I loved to join the Jesuits, which only amplified my joy and fervor for service. As I look to the second half of my life, I admire more senior Jesuits who know when the time is right to let go of work or ministry they love and retire to different kinds of service. A wise and very free Jesuit mentor once told me, "We older folks must leave room for younger people to lead and show the way." I also have been with many parents of first-year college students as they dropped their grown children off at school. There is a moment, usually full of tears, when they hug their son or daughter and then let go, getting in the car, driving back to a quiet, emptier home, and giving space for their child to grow into the person God calls them to be.

Letting go is hard, because we usually experience some emptiness, even loneliness. But if we have the courage to persist, and not rush to grasp something else to fill the uncomfortable or painful void, then we usually realize an unexpected gift: the parent develops a more adult relationship with a child; a new kind of work offers surprising fulfillment and summons latent talents in us; retirement offers peace and deepened relationships we never realized we needed. To hold on too tightly to someone or something is what Ignatius means by an attachment, a love, that becomes disordered. Close or clench your hands into a fist: this is what a disordered attachment looks and feels like. Now, open your hands, and turn your palms up. Your hands are empty, yet also open to receive something new, some unexpected gift.

We can practice freedom in other ordinary ways. We stand up to peer pressure. We call out a racist comment. We let go of resentments, which only end up hurting us. We befriend someone whom others shun. We forgive another person for a past hurt. We refrain from work to allow for some rest. We save water easily wasted. We enjoy a nourishing solitude rather than run from it.

The more we practice freedom in small ways, the freer we become, and in my experience, free people are really great to be around. I am at ease around them and learn from them. In such company, I am a better person. Pope Francis offers a word of advice, especially to the young: seek out the company of grandparents and other elder wisdom figures. By befriending and listening to them, we "learn their secret, the secret that has allowed them to navigate their way through the adventure of life" and receive "the wisdom of people who have not only stayed the course over time but who have maintained gratitude in their hearts for everything they have experienced." Their freedom can be contagious if we are open to it.

Interior freedom is a fantastic feeling, delightful to savor. In freedom, we enjoy a homecoming celebration of sorts and embrace more festivity in our lives. At the same time, the point of becoming free is to do something with that freedom. Otherwise, all this taking stock and clearing the rubble from our hearts is a U-turn back to self-preoccupation and isolation. Too often, talking about sin leads to self-inflicted punishment rather than freeing ourselves for service and building community.

In this chapter, we have recognized how we are sometimes like the prodigal son and his older brother, but we can also become like the father, the one who loves so generously because he is so free. In the Gospels, at the beginning of his public ministry, Jesus is baptized in the Jordan River, and he hears a voice from the heavens: "You are my beloved Son; with you I am well pleased" (Mark 1:9–11). This is a moment of great consolation for Jesus and provides him with clarity about his mission and who he is becoming. He easily could have rested on the banks of the Jordan and just basked in the glow of his Father's love. Instead, he steps out of the Jordan and gets to work, building God's reign of justice, peace, and love. Empowered by the love he received from his Father in heaven, Jesus spends the rest of his days showing people how beloved they are, especially those whom society had pushed to the margins.

If we are quiet and still enough, we loved sinners or beautifully flawed people can hear that same whisper: "You are my beloved, with you I am well pleased." These words can sink deep down into our rubbled-over hearts and free us to do amazing things. Or liberation may come after a cannonball moment like Ignatius's when our world is rocked and the ground shifts under our feet. Whether through a gentle call or a jarring experience, we reach a point of decision: do we accept the invitation to greater freedom, letting go of little dreams to embrace larger ones, leaving behind our familiar but disordered attachments to enjoy greater loves? If we dare to say yes to the invitation, we return home from our distant country, eager to join the feast and hopefully bringing others along with us.

## SPIRITUAL EXERCISES

- Find a quiet time and space to reflect on the following questions: Where or how do I experience freedom in my life? Where or how do I experience unfreedom? Who are the free people in my life? What qualities define them?

- Pray with your hands, alternating between a clenched fist and open palms. What disordered attachments am I clinging to? What do I need to let go of? What hopes do I have in my posture of openness and availability?

- Consider the image of a rubbled-over heart: What names do you give the stones around your heart? Consider the biblical image of the devil as the father of lies: Which lies are easy for you to believe? What truth do you need to embrace to set you free?

- As you reflect on your life, what are those chief sins (or weaknesses) that give rise to other sins? Fear? Ingratitude? Failure to acknowledge your goodness or the goodness of another?

- Consider a cannonball moment in your life. How do you make sense of it or find meaning in it from the viewpoint of freedom?

## Chapter 5

# LIVING OUT OF GREAT DESIRES
## The Virtue of Magnanimity

Just five months before graduating, Brandon dropped by my office to share the news: he had decided not to pursue well-placed consulting jobs in New York and Washington, as he had planned, and was instead heading to Los Angeles to pursue a career in acting. He knew others would think he was crazy for taking such an unorthodox and risky path, but he needed to do this, at least give it a try, because he realized he would regret it if he didn't. Having given up baseball after an injury, Brandon grew to love drama and performance in college. He got the same rush acting as he did playing competitive sports. This passion, which seemed like a diversion at first, became a vocation, a calling.

I think Brandon came to me for some validation because he knew my own story. I had given up a law practice to teach high school and then ultimately enter the Jesuits. I had become comfortable with the unorthodox path. We talked through his decision. He understood the risks and was clearheaded about how competitive it would be in LA. He also was able to articulate, or at least begin to name, deeper desires that impelled him to choose this path. Brandon recognized in a healthy way how ego, or the need for affirmation of the crowd, might be playing into the desire to perform, but his greater and more sincere desire tapped into a life-giving, creative side of him. I explained that most of us wrestle with mixed motivations, so it was important to let the more noble ambitions drive him.

Ultimately, it was Brandon's decision to make, not mine, and I assured him of my support along the way. As I tried to encourage him, the words of the poet Rilke ran through my head. Asked by a younger poet what he should do, Rilke replied:

> This most of all: ask yourself in the most silent hour of your night: must I write? Dig into yourself for a deep answer. And if this answer rings out in assent, if you meet this solemn question with a strong, simple "I must," then build your life in accordance with this necessity; your whole life, even into its humblest and most indifferent hour, must become a sign and witness to this impulse.

In the deepest places of our heart, we find God's voice within. For too long, the Christian tradition ran away from desire as temptation that leads us wildly astray. The Dominican theologian Timothy Radcliffe observes: "Most people think of religion as about the control of desire. Desire is dangerous and disturbing and so religion helps us tame it. But traditionally this has not been the teaching of the Church. We are invited to deepen our desires, to touch their hidden hunger, to liberate desire in recognition of its ultimate goal," which is God, both the source and the ultimate fulfillment of our longing.

Ignatius helped to redeem desire in the Christian tradition by casting desire as natural and God-given, and thus fundamentally good. In 1551, Ignatius wrote to the Jesuits at their newly established college in Ferrara, Italy. Instructing them on their ministry there, Ignatius began with this counsel: "They should endeavor to conceive great resolves and elicit equally great desires to be true and faithful servants of God." Desires constitute part of the restlessness we experience as human beings. In the Ignatian view of the human person, what we most deeply want reflects what God most deeply wants for us because God is the one who placed those deep desires in us in the first place: that's why we can call these desires "holy." Our deepest desires reflect the heart of God.

Ignatius believed that God communicates with us through these desires, just as we can discern God's voice in our thinking and feeling. Desires, as we well know, are powerful and complicated stuff, so we are wise to ask where they come from and where they lead us. Desires are another one of those currents on the river that move us along. We need to sort through those desires, and other interior movements, to ensure that they are indeed good and holy, leading us to the shore we are aiming for. Paying attention to them is the first step in navigating them well, following the desires that are life giving and healthy and avoiding those that will send us crashing into the riverbank.

For example, we can distinguish those desires that are superficial and fleeting from those that are deep and lasting. There is nothing wrong with surface desires—they are a part of who we are—but we can choose to sacrifice satisfying those desires in order to honor deeper desires that are more self-defining or fundamental for us. As my friends know well, I *love* chocolate, but I choose to share some of my chocolate with a friend because my desire for friendship is deeper than my desire for chocolate. Deep and holy desires reflect who we are and who we want to be—or who God calls us to be. Honoring them helps us make and sustain fundamental commitments in our life.

As I sat with Brandon through his discernment, I wanted to be sure that he was not going to LA because it was the more adventurous path, which can be a particular temptation for young people. Sometimes, the glib advice to "follow your passion" gets reduced to "take the road less traveled." This simplistic approach, though, short-circuits discernment, which is so central to the Ignatian tradition, the rudder that helps us negotiate all those currents in the river. My path was to leave the practice of law; for others, the law may be the road they are called to follow. Discernment means that we take seriously our life experience with all its complexity. We dig into ourselves, as Rilke wrote, for the deep answer. We want to make sure the object of our desire—where we want to go and what we want to do—truly reflects who we are, with all our other commitments, and who God calls us to be. Put another way, we want to ensure that our desires align with our purpose, what we described earlier as our first principle and foundation.

In this chapter, we explore the centrality of desires in the Ignatian tradition and how those desires, once tapped, must be discerned, honed, and then offered in service to others. We will see how living out of our deepest desires is an expression of the virtue of magnanimity, or generosity, and how humility complements that virtue. As you read, consider how your own desires have taken shape over your lifetime, and where they may be pointing you now, at this moment of your journey.

# Striving for the Magis

Earlier we described Ignatius's conversion as turning away from unfreedoms so that he could be free for greater service to God and others. The work of discerning our deep desires reflects a similar kind of turning. Authentic freedom animates great, holy desires in us. We turn inward to notice and sift through these desires: no one else can do that soul-searching for us. At the same time, we do not want to get stuck in endless self-examination; otherwise, we are just navel gazing and can easily lapse into self-involvement. We ultimately need to turn outward. Having named and refined our deepest and truest desires, we then act on them to serve God and others; this is the Ignatian turn.

To make this turn, or conversion of self, from looking inward to looking outward, Ignatius relies on the virtue of magnanimity (SE 5). This is an ancient virtue that essentially means largeness of heart, or greatness of soul. The medieval philosopher and theologian Thomas Aquinas explained that magnanimity "makes a [person] deem himself worthy of great things in consideration of the gifts he holds from God." In other words, in the truly magnanimous person, we find a well-cultivated sense of gratitude: gratitude for what we have received fuels our desire to give back, to do "great things."

In his writings, Ignatius relied on a phrase so often that it became the unofficial motto of the Jesuits, familiar to students and alumni of Jesuit schools around the world: *ad majorem Dei gloriam,* translated from Latin to English as "for the greater glory of God." (In Jesuit ministries today, this motto is often abbreviated as AMDG.) In the Constitutions that Ignatius composed for the Jesuits as a religious order, the AMDG appears in some form 376 times. All that Jesuits and their colleagues do must be directed to the greater glory of God. Magnanimity urges us not to settle for mediocrity but to strive for the "greater": to serve God and our neighbor *more* fully or do what will *better* serve the common good. Serving the greater glory of God does *not* mean that God needs us to stroke the divine ego! To the contrary, in the words of second-century theologian Irenaeus, the glory of God is the human person fully alive. By honoring our deep and holy desires, we bring life to those we serve, but we also become more fully alive as we realize the person God desires us to be.

In the past few decades, a new Jesuit term of art emerged that tries to capture the meaning of the AMDG: *magis*. Originally an adverb in Latin meaning "more" or "to a greater degree," *magis* today is often used as a noun in Jesuit-related circles, such as "strive for the *magis*." In 1995, at a meeting of Jesuits from around the world, called a General Congregation, the Jesuits described the *magis* in a way that characterizes the magnanimous person:

> The *magis* is not simply one among others in a list of Jesuit characteristics. It permeates them all. The entire life of Ignatius was a pilgrim search for the *magis*, the ever greater glory of God, the ever fuller service of our neighbor, the more universal good, the more effective apostolic means. . . . Jesuits are never content with the status quo, the known, the tried, the already existing. We are constantly driven to discover, redefine, and reach out for the *magis*. For us, frontiers and boundaries are not obstacles or ends, but new challenges to be faced, new opportunities to be welcomed. Indeed, ours is a holy boldness.

The *magis* taps into our restlessness to make the world a more just and gentle place. It stirs up passionate, holy desires to spend our lives for the good of others in a way that does not diminish us but instead leads to our flourishing. The *magis* also means that we need to summon courage as we face and overcome the obstacles that arise when we try to achieve "great things."

# Naming Our Deep Desires

Jesus knew the power of desire to transform people and societies. As we saw in an earlier chapter, Jesus loved asking questions as a way of building and deepening relationships and honoring the autonomy of the people he encountered. Bartimaeus was one of those people. Usually, the Gospels do not offer the names of the people Jesus helps; that we know Bartimaeus's name tells us that this encounter was particularly significant. According to Mark's Gospel, Bartimaeus, who is blind, is sitting and begging by the road near Jericho when Jesus and a crowd of people walk by. Hearing it is Jesus, Bartimaeus yells, "Jesus, Son of David, have pity on me." The crowd tries to shut him up, but Bartimaeus persists, crying out, "Son of David, have pity on me." Jesus stops, calls Bartimaeus to his side, and asks: "What do you want me to do for you?" Enthusiastically rushing to Jesus' side, Bartimaeus replies: "Master, I want to see." And Jesus does so: "Your faith has saved you." Once healed, Bartimaeus joins the others and follows Jesus (Mark 10:46–52).

We can reasonably ask why Jesus would even need to ask Bartimaeus what he wants. His blindness would be apparent from his behavior, appearance, or the crowd's murmuring. But for Jesus, healing is relational, not transactional. As a man with a physical infirmity, Bartimaeus lived in peril, forced to beg because there was no social safety net like the ones so many people rely on today. Equally distressing, he would have suffered from social ostracism, since in his context, society would have presumed that his infirmity was a sign that he or his family had done something wrong. By inviting him into relationship, Jesus subverted those social expectations. By asking him what he wanted, Jesus also empowered Bartimaeus, who was so marginalized in his society. As the crowd tried to silence him, Jesus gave him a voice. Through spoken and unspoken word, Bartimaeus said: "I want to see. I want to be part of the community again. I want my suffering to end. I want my dignity back. I want to follow you." Beneath his desire to have his sight restored lay a host of other deeper desires.

Bartimaeus is a model for us as we try to identify and voice our own deep desires. Articulating what we *really* want, finding the deep answer, is not always easy. Even if we fumble for words, voicing our longings helps us understand them and claim them as our own. For those who have been told that their voice is not important or that their desires are not significant, naming desires is empowering, as it was for Bartimaeus. Finally, if we ask for what we want and are later given it, then we can be thankful to God and others who helped us realize the promise inherent in those desires. Such appreciation serves only to deepen bonds of affection with God and others.

Throughout the Exercises, Ignatius urges us to keep naming what we want. Each time you begin to pray, he writes, "ask God our Lord for what [you] want and desire" (SE 48). In other words, respond to the question Jesus posed to Bartimaeus: *What do you want me to do for you?* Or to the question Jesus posed to the first disciples, whom we met earlier in the book: *What are you looking for?* Ignatius even suggests graces or gifts to ask for, for example, joy, compassion, sorrow for sins, generosity, insight or understanding, good judgment, and deepening knowledge of Jesus. These are all worthy petitions, but we are free to depart from Ignatius's suggestions to give voice to particular desires that may be emerging in us. As Ignatius writes at the beginning of the Exercises, God works with each person and each person's particular circumstances (SE 15). Such flexibility is part of the genius of the Exercises. Ignatius trusted God and the person making the Exercises to find their way together.

# Responding to the Call to Build a More Just and Gentle World

In addition to the repeated practice of asking for what we want when we are praying, Ignatius offers an extended exercise that frames our deep desires as a response to an invitation from Jesus to join him in realizing God's reign of justice, peace, and love (SE 91–98). In a key meditation in the Spiritual Exercises, Ignatius first suggests that we imagine an earthly ruler who inspires us to join a noble cause. In his time, Ignatius naturally thought of royal figures. When making this exercise, I contemporize Ignatius's invitation. I have thought about political or civic figures who have inspired me, like Robert Kennedy, Dorothy Day, Nelson Mandela, and Martin Luther King Jr. I have also thought about people in my own life who have inspired me by their service to others and their commitment to justice.

Sister Katherine Nueslein of the Sisters of Mercy is for me one of those guiding examples. In my second year as a Jesuit novice, I was sent to Southwest Baltimore to work with her. This meant doing lots of walking around the neighborhood where she lived and worked, one where people struggled and lived in poverty. She had started a number of community-based service organizations, including a learning center for adults with developmental disabilities and a program to redevelop housing in the blighted area. It was a hot and humid summer, typical of Baltimore, so Kitty (as she was affectionately known) and I did a lot of talking on the shaded doorstep of her modest rowhouse. With the Georgia accent she never lost, Kitty could talk with anyone, and she did, at length! She listened intently too and was masterful in gently cajoling someone to help, and firmly calling out someone trying to scam her, but without being alienating. No one was outside of her care. Her ministry was tough, as was dealing with some church officials who were not used to working with such a strong woman. Her sense of humor raised spirits and defused difficult situations.

Toward the end of our summer together, Kitty, around sixty-five at the time, suffered a minor heart attack and was uncharacteristically out of commission for a few weeks. So, I filled in for her where I could, running kids across the city to a community pool to escape the summer's heat and preaching at a local Baptist church during an ecumenical prayer service. She laughed easily as I shared the latest gossip from the neighborhood, where I continued to walk. When I returned to Syracuse to profess my first vows as a Jesuit, she gave me a cross that she used to wear around her traditional nun's habit (which she had not worn for decades). "I'm supposed to be buried with this, but what use is it to me then," she told me with a smile. "I would rather give it to someone who will carry on the work to help people others forget." Kitty died in 2010, more than a decade after we first met.

Throughout my Jesuit life, Kitty's cross has hung next to the crucifix I was given when I professed my vows, both reminders of what my vocation as a Jesuit and honorary Sister of Mercy (as Kitty dubbed me!) is all about. I hope to give both away before I die.

Regardless of who your inspiring earthly leader is, the key is to think of someone who stirs up in you a passion to make the world more good, beautiful, and just. Then, Ignatius asks rhetorically: "If such a summons of an earthly king to his subjects deserves our attention, how much more worthy of consideration is Christ our Lord, the Eternal King, before whom is assembled the whole world" (SE 95). Or we might say: just as our contemporary servant leaders inspire us to follow them, how much more does Jesus inspire us to advance his reign of justice, peace, and love and to make his cause our own?

Ignatius then invites us, now inspired, to hear Jesus calling us in these words: "Whoever wishes to join me in this enterprise must be willing to labor with me, that by following me in suffering, [they] may follow me in glory" (SE 95). This invitation is both provocative and brutally honest. Provocative, because Jesus invites us to partner with him in the work ahead, laboring "with me." In Jesus, we meet a messiah, a leader, who does not mind asking for help, and for whom partnership is itself a glimpse of the reign of God he wishes to promote. The invitation is also honest, because it recognizes that building a reign of justice, peace, and love is not easy and will bring pain and resistance, as the lives of Jesus and many world leaders attest. Still, the call enlarges our heart, stirring up in us a magnanimous response. When I use my imagination to bring to life Jesus' call in this exercise, I hear words like those of Teddy Roosevelt, speaking at the Sorbonne in France in 1910:

> It is not the critic who counts; not the man who points out how the strong man stumbles or where the doer of deeds could have done them better. The credit belongs to the man who is actually in the arena, whose face is marred by dust and sweat and blood; who strives valiantly; who errs, who comes short again

and again, because there is no effort without error and short-
coming; but who does actually strive to do the deeds; who knows
the great enthusiasms, the great devotions; who spends himself
in a worthy cause; who at the best knows in the end the triumph
of high achievement, and who at the worst, if he fails, at least
fails while daring greatly, so that his place shall never be with
those cold and timid souls who neither know victory nor defeat.

In praying through this meditation on the kingdom or reign of Jesus Christ,
Ignatius asks us to assess our interior reactions to the call to build a more
just and gentle world: Do you notice any great desires being stirred within
you? Do you notice any resistances, like fear, percolating? Are you hesitant
at all? If so, does the invitation at least attract you in some way? Go into
yourself, as Rilke advised, and pay attention to your deep desires, whether
they are like flames already burning strongly or embers waiting to be stirred.

Ignatius places his meditation on the call of Jesus Christ at a turning point
in the Spiritual Exercises. As we discussed earlier, the person making the
Exercises reflects on their unfreedoms or sin and their need for God's mercy
or encouragement. Hopefully, they experience that mercy as a profound
acceptance of themselves as a sinner or broken human being who is beautifully created and loved unconditionally. This radical acceptance is transformative. Having had this deeply personal, even visceral experience of mercy
and acceptance, people naturally want to share that mercy with others. Their
desire for something more—the *magis*—is stirred. Freedom breeds great
desires. At this crucial moment, they hear this call, and they naturally want
to follow or contribute to making God's dream for the world a reality. This is
the "honeymoon phase" for the disciple. They may not fully appreciate how
hard the road may get, but they know it is worth traveling.

# Making Sense of Evolving Desires

Deep desires are rarely static. They evolve as we evolve or grow up, one
desire leading to another. With the wisdom that comes with age and

experience, we also get better at articulating our desires. We embrace our restlessness rather than run away from it. We keep looking for the deep answer, the desire beneath the desire: *What do I really want? What am I looking for?* We notice how the desires that initially animated our journey are deepening or changing in some way, or how other desires are emerging as we live, learn, and love in new ways.

Looking back at my life, I can trace in broad strokes my desire to serve as a Jesuit. Growing up, I knew I wanted to do something that would help others, a desire instilled in me by my faith and family. I thought I would serve in law and public office. But then, when I was practicing law, I was invited to teach high school. I initially declined, content to stay on the career track I had devised years before. But the invitation kept nagging at me. I found myself imagining life as a teacher and getting excited about it. My desires grew. I left my law practice to teach, which only stoked in me other desires. I found a calling as an educator: I loved teaching and was good at it. Yet I was still restless, and I allowed myself to consider something I had briefly thought about in college: becoming a Jesuit. I wanted to help young people and their families not only as a teacher but also as a priest.

Just as love in a committed relationship deepens and expands, ebbs and flows, my desires as a Jesuit priest have evolved. As a younger Jesuit, I was asked to help out for a summer in immigration detention centers in Los Angeles. Peter Neeley, the Jesuit priest assigned to the detention centers, needed a break, so I filled in for him for a summer. That experience would go on to spark in me an unexpected and lifelong commitment to advocate for migrants, refugees, and first-generation college students—a vocation within a vocation.

Besides dealing with the mind-numbing bureaucracy of working in US jails and prisons, Peter's orientation to me was brief when I asked him what I should do when he was away: just listen to them, and walk with them. I did the listening mostly in the common area, a recreation room with metal seats and tables, bright, florescent overhead lights, and a TV blaring in the corner. There, I met sons, daughters, and parents living the painful stories of separation and desperation that I had first heard in Mexico when I was a Jesuit novice a few years earlier. One mother told me she was being deported back to Mexico, leaving behind children who had the good fortune of being born in the United States. A man who had lived in the US for two decades and had raised a family here was being deported after he had been pulled over for a minor traffic violation. A younger man, just over eighteen, assured me he would try again to cross the border because he had no choice: his family back in Honduras needed the money he could earn in the US as a laborer in the fields of central California. A transgender woman told me she could not stay in her home country because she would be abused or killed (while in detention, she was kept in isolation to protect her). The walking part of my job description took place in "the yard," an outdoor recreation area surrounded by high concrete walls. When the wind blew easterly, I could smell the salty ocean air from the nearby Pacific Ocean, a tantalizing aroma of freedom.

Sparked by my summer experience in Los Angeles, I later wrote my graduate thesis on the theological underpinnings of the work of the Jesuit Refugee Service, founded in 1980 to accompany, serve, and advocate for refugees and migrants around the world. On the days when I struggled to organize my research or ran into writer's block, I kept my desires alive by remembering the people I met in LA. I carry with me two gifts from men I met in detention: a penciled sketch of the Virgin of Guadalupe, a common devotion of migrants from Mexico and Central America, and a rose made of twisted toilet paper, both positioned prominently at my desk. Later, as a college educator, I prioritized getting to know and supporting first-generation and undocumented college students. Fr. Neeley's counsel remains the same: listen to them, walk with them. When I do, my desires are shaped and deepened for greater service, including most recently joining efforts to expand access to Jesuit higher education by opening a two-year junior college on the East Coast.

Attentive to how my own vocation story has unfolded, I am better able to understand and guide younger people as they discern their desires. Michelle's story provides an example of desires that evolved along a fairly straight path (at least for now). From a young age, Michelle loved writing. In high school, she developed a strong interest in journalism and earned an internship covering breaking news at her hometown newspaper, the *Miami Herald*. There she learned how reporting could hold political leaders accountable and highlight issues important to her, like racial justice. Michelle struggled at times because her family did not initially endorse her career path, and she did not see many journalists who looked like her, a Black woman. In college, she wrote for a school newspaper and got an internship at the *Washington Post*.

As Michelle approached graduation from college, she came to me because she had to sort through various career choices. She had several opportunities in more traditional and more lucrative fields of business. She was also considering law school, a common ambition among her class-mates. Yet she could not ignore her deeper desire to uplift people and bring injustices to light as a journalist. She committed to a path reflective of her deeply felt calling, first in print and then in broadcast journalism. Along the way, she found people of color in her profession to guide and support her. As she grew in the competitive field of journalism in New York and Wash-ington, DC, Michelle refused to let the naysayers extinguish her passion. Today, she is a prominent broadcast journalist and mentors young people with similar passions for journalism.

Her vocation as a journalist continues to unfold, one choice evolving into another. To make sure she is honoring her inner compass, she prays regularly, incorporating the practice of the Examen (which we discussed earlier in the book). In a recent conversation, she told me: "I try to align myself with God's purpose for my life, and not more superficial concerns. I don't want to lose myself as I advance in my career."

Other vocation stories, like my own, take roads with more bends and turns than Michelle's. Brandon headed to LA to give acting a try, but after a year or so, he decided he did not have the drive to compete and succeed in Hollywood over the long run. As Brandon recently explained to me, "I real-ized at one point, 'I don't love this enough to need to do it.'" He recounted one moment that crystalized his discernment. Like most aspiring actors in

LA, he waited tables at night to pay the bills. At one event, he worked with another actor who was about twenty years older than Brandon and had a young daughter. While serving, Brandon's friend relied on a cane because he could not afford surgery to repair an injury. At one point, he dropped a tray of food, causing a commotion. Innately sympathetic, Brandon helped his friend. While doing so, he knew deep down that this part of his journey was over. Always desiring to be a father, Brandon wanted to provide more security to his future family than acting provided him.

Ironically, given my own career direction, Brandon ultimately went to a prestigious law school and is practicing law in New York and raising a family. Brandon has no regrets about giving acting a try (as I don't regret my time practicing law) because along the way, he learned a great deal about himself, lessons that continue to serve him well today. He has come to appreciate how much acting makes him a better trial lawyer. Brandon crafts more persuasive arguments to a judge and jury, "reads" them as he would an audience, and improvises amid the drama of the courtroom. By his own admission, amid all the demands of family and career, Brandon has let his creative side atrophy a bit, and he is looking for ways to keep stirring the embers of this desire. He is also trying to better balance his vocation as a lawyer with his vocation as husband and father. Given that we have limited time and energy, finding this balance is hard, but Brandon has prioritized his vocation as husband and father, which helps him make choices.

My good friend Kurt and I entered the Jesuit order on the same day. We "grew up" together in the Society, sharing many meaningful, fun, and challenging experiences along the way. In many respects, Jesuit life and mission fit Kurt. Yet after many years, and despite successfully completing numerous Jesuit assignments and engaging in a ministry that proved fruitful and life giving to others, Kurt found himself struggling with deep loneliness and a draw to pursue other profound desires. He took the commitment he had made very seriously, but also valued Jesuit life and ministry too highly to live them out with anything less than 100 percent of his whole self.

After a lot of prayerful discernment and consultation, Kurt decided to leave the Jesuits. Importantly, as with any discernment—but especially one that implicates larger questions of service, meaning, and mission—Kurt made his decision only when it was clear to him and to those accompanying him that his decision was not about just "leaving the Jesuits," the way one might leave a tough job or move to a more desirable city. Kurt was at peace with his decision only when it became clear that it was an affirmative response to deeply existential desires—in his case, for marriage and father-hood and a continued life of service, albeit in a different form. He knew those desires were significant and could be trusted as being of God because they lingered, clearly and persistently, and because they remained consis-tent with the underlying desires that had led him to the Jesuits—namely, living a commitment for and with others, animated by a spirit of giving back to the world, especially to those most in need.

Becoming a Jesuit was not a mistake for Kurt. Far from it: he did much good as a Jesuit and continues to do so as a layman. Kurt now has a won-derful family and runs a nonprofit organization providing legal aid to those who cannot afford a lawyer. He says happily that all that he learned and experienced as a Jesuit freed him to love and be loved as a husband and father and to engage in a profession of service to others in ways that he could not have imagined before joining the Jesuits. Authentic discernment is a dynamic, "long view" phenomenon that cannot be restricted to a par-ticular point in life or a singular decision. Kurt practiced discernment across the arc of his life, helping him make a series of life decisions amid the com-plexity and unpredictability that life entails, all in partnership with the God who created him and who still creates in and through him.

## Refining Our Desires

Whether our river is straight or winding, well traveled or uncharted, God stays with us. God never says: "Wrong turn! See you later after you figure out how to get yourself out of the mess you created!" To the contrary, God is faithful, which I think also sums up the Bible in a few words. A sign of that faithful, divine presence are the deep desires that God gives us as a way to get us where we need to go. Those desires are also a reminder that we are not alone on the journey.

I have always considered myself a passionate person, so I was surprised when I encountered a phase in my life when my desires for ministry and for living a Jesuit life did not simply change but stagnated. Sometimes a persistent loss of desire can indicate that we need to change course: maybe change our work or adjust how we are living. With the help of a good therapist and a wise spiritual director, I identified some underlying disillusionment and hurt that sapped my desires of their vitality. Gradually, and sometimes painfully, I learned to deal with those underlying emotions. Rather than freaking out, I also accepted that such dry seasons happen in life, as many married couples face in their relationship, or anyone does in a career. God is faithful, and we can return that faithfulness in dry seasons when it is tempting to ignore or run away from dissipating desires. Looking back now, I was going through some spiritual growing pains. That my desires felt different did not mean that they were not deep or holy. They were still a source of life for me, just in a different way. Although I initially felt that I was alone, I realized that I was being invited to spend time with God in a new and surprising way, different from what I was used to.

Even when we are easily in touch with our God-given desires, we might need to refine them so that they do not get us off track. Ignatius was a man of great passion and high ideals, but he learned early that he needed to hone or better direct his bold desires, lest they deter him. During the months of his initial conversion, he was so enthusiastic about his new path in life that he wanted to outperform the feats of the saints who inspired him, and he went to extremes with his devotions and penances. Ignatius ultimately figured out that these ambitions were too self-involved and ultimately exercises in vanity. Growth came slowly for the future saint, a consoling thought for the rest of us who don't get it right all the time. Ignatius eventually heeded the advice of spiritual mentors who directed him to find more balance in his life. He began to focus his desires so that his passion would not remain so diffuse that it would be wasted.

Working with young people, I have found Ignatius's story compelling. Thank God, young people (and many older people!) want to change the world. Their enthusiasm is contagious. Captured by God's dream for the world, many want to work for greater racial, social, and environmental justice. However, if such desires are not refined, we face two related risks that can undermine our noble efforts. First, we can easily burn out and become disillusioned if we do not make the progress we seek, in the time we have determined. Second, we can unintentionally develop a Messiah complex, thinking "nothing can be accomplished without me" and "I can do great things all by myself and better than everyone else."

Such temptations are a corruption of the *magis*. Stretching for what is more or greater should not lead us to workaholism, burnout, pride, or perfectionism. The *magis* does not necessarily mean doing more, giving more, or spending more time on something; it does not even mean that we are successful. Striving for the *magis* means doing what God gives us to do as best we can, with a generous or magnanimous heart. The *magis* is an approach to *how* we do things more than a list of things to do or a litany of accomplishments.

## Wrestling with Unfulfilled Desires

In my ministry as a priest, one of the most challenging and frequent questions I get is why God does not satisfy our deep desires when we so sincerely, even desperately, ask that they be satisfied. We hear Jesus' question to Bartimaeus, "What do you want me to do for you?" We respond honestly and unequivocally: "I want to get married," "I want to have children," "I want to be reconciled with my friend," "I want *that* job." After responding, we wait, and we wait, and then . . . nothing. This is maddening and painful. Pious platitudes ("It's God's will") and empty guarantees ("You will find the right person") only make it worse. The most important thing any of us can do when someone else is in that situation is to affirm that person's desire as holy and good and any pain as human and real. We walk with that person in their questions, confusion, sadness, or anger.

How do we make sense of this frustration of desire? The spiritual tradition offers a few perspectives that may be helpful.

**First, God may be giving us what we are asking for but in ways we do not fully recognize or notice.** For example, in our desire for a romantic relationship or more meaningful work, we might be overlooking a person already present in our lives or be dismissing too quickly a career opportunity before us (as I did when I initially turned down the offer to teach high school). In such cases, we are called to be creative or pay more attention to the details of our experiences.

**Second, although we may not be getting what we *want*, God may be giving us what we *need* at the moment.** I thank God for unanswered prayers that were voiced in haste or shortsightedness or unfreedom. I recall wanting a particular job so much and being disappointed when I did not get it. Only later did I realize the blessing of that outcome: I would have been miserable. In these cases, patience is a helpful virtue to cultivate, as is humility: we do not have all the answers or the perspective we sometimes need.

**Third, we may not be ready for what God wants to give us.** Recall St. Augustine's beautiful recognition that our hearts are restless until they rest in God. The patron saint of restless hearts, Augustine offered this response to the problem of unfulfilled desire: "The entire life of a good Christian is an exercise in holy desire. . . . Simply by making us wait God increases our desire, which in turn enlarges the capacity of the soul, making it able to receive what is to be given to us." Patience is needed so our desires can expand with time. Timothy Radcliffe summarizes Augustine's insight: "God sometimes hangs back so as to teach us to desire more. . . . We are like bags that need to be stretched to become big enough for what God wishes to give."

**Fourth, we need to be realistic.** We follow our passions amid certain commitments and realities. A generous, deeply committed college graduate really wants to join the Peace Corps but decides to take a well-paying job in order to pay off student loans. A talented son declines a "dream job" in another city in order to care for his ailing mother. Both are reasonable and principled decisions in the context of these particular situations (other people may reach different conclusions). Those decisions may simply delay, rather than deny, the realization of their deep desire. Or these individuals may discover other ways to honor their deep desires and develop their God-given talents: the college graduate may volunteer time at a not-for-profit after work; the devoted son may find enriching opportunities closer to home; a couple who cannot conceive a child may discover the joy of adoption.

**Fifth, our desires may not be compatible with the desires expressed by others.** A young person falls in love, but the object of their affection does not share the same romantic feelings. The free will and personal autonomy that we enjoy as human beings make this sad outcome as possible as the joyful consequence of love freely returned. Moreover, freedom can be misused or abused. Consider, for example, how a magnanimous person may have his or her career path impeded by the personal bias of another or by unjust policies or laws. When this happens, authentic and holy desires run up against the sinful dispositions and hurtful actions of others. This requires resilience on the part of the person whose desires are being thwarted; it also calls on others to stand with that person in countering injustice, clearing the path as much as possible for their flourishing, and thereby the flourishing of the community.

## Balancing Magnanimity with Humility

Even as we tap into our God-given desires and imagine doing "great things," we also need to be willing to decenter ourselves in two other ways: by letting others join us in our noble project and by sacrificing short-term fulfillment for longer-term gain. This kind of humble decentering is beautifully captured in a prayer offered in 1979 by Cardinal John Dearden of Detroit, more recently shared again by Pope Francis in 2015:

> It helps, now and then, to step back and take a long view.
> The kingdom is not only beyond our efforts, it is even beyond
>     our vision.
> We accomplish in our lifetime only a tiny fraction

of the magnificent enterprise that is God's work.

Nothing we do is complete,

which is a way of saying that

the Kingdom always lies beyond us.

No statement says all that could be said.

No prayer fully expresses our faith.

No confession brings perfection.

No pastoral visit brings wholeness.

No program accomplishes the Church's mission.

No set of goals and objectives includes everything.

This is what we are about.

We plant the seeds that one day will grow.

We water seeds already planted, knowing that they hold future
     promise.

We lay foundations that will need further development.

We provide yeast that produces far beyond our capabilities.

We cannot do everything, and there is a sense of liberation in
     realizing that.

This enables us to do something, and to do it very well.

It may be incomplete, but it is a beginning, a step along the
     way,

An opportunity for the Lord's grace to enter and do the rest.

We may never see the end results, but that is the difference
     between the master builder and the worker.

We are workers, not master builders; ministers, not messiahs.

We are prophets of a future not our own.

In making this prayer our own, the challenge is to decenter ourselves without diminishing ourselves, to be much-needed prophets without becoming obnoxious messiahs. As I was discerning whether to become a Jesuit, I was very attracted to the magnanimity I saw in Jesuits I knew. They were passionate, alive in their ministry, and focused on helping people and laboring for justice. As I have shared, when I was younger, I aspired to a career in law and politics. Some of this was youthful, ego-centered ambition, but I also sincerely wanted to do great things to help people. I discerned that instead of offering that service in politics, I would serve as a Jesuit and priest.

My formation as a Jesuit helped me embrace God-given passions and understand how I could best serve others, as an educator, spiritual director, priest, and administrative leader. Tapping into those desires, I felt fully alive when teaching, leading retreats, preaching, and motivating people in a shared mission. All this is good, but I increasingly became concerned that I was becoming too proud or vain, so I started to defer opportunities to lead, and I actually downplayed my talents. A wise spiritual director pointed out that I was overcorrecting. In the Spiritual Exercises, and in his own experience, Ignatius imagined that such a temptation to false humility would visit good people who were becoming more magnanimous. Fearing that they will become too proud or self-centered, they instead become timid in offering their gifts in the service of others. "In such cases," Ignatius advised, "one should raise his mind to his Creator and Lord, and if he sees that what he is about to do is in keeping with God's service, or at least not opposed to it, he should act directly against the temptation" (SE 351).

My approach—don't do anything!—was too simple, even immature. Ignatian spirituality treats us like adults, inviting us to embrace nuance and complexity and do the hard work of discerning the often complicated terrain of our interior life. In this case, I needed to honor bold and holy desires in a spirit of magnanimity while at the same time cultivating the virtue of humility. A truly humble person is grounded in the reality of who they are, and whose they are. We are not God (thank God!), and we do not need to save the world, only try to make it better.

In humility, we recognize that we cannot achieve "great things" without God's help and the help of other people. In gratitude, we acknowledge our gifts, strengths, and accomplishments, and gracefully accept compliments while recognizing God as the giver of all good gifts.

We also need to cultivate humility because we might fail in our attempt to do "great things." Realistic in striving for the *magis*, we can stumble without our world falling apart because we, to use Teddy Roosevelt's words, spend ourselves in a worthy cause and fail while daring greatly. As both magnanimous and humble, we recognize that the "great things" we seek to accomplish are not for our self-glorification but for God's greater glory—that is, for whatever furthers God's reign of justice, peace, and love.

# Reconsidering "Greatness"

Ignatian spirituality elicits great desires in people so that they can better serve others. In our hypercompetitive culture, greatness can take on different meanings. At points in my life, when I was energized to do great things, I thought that meant engaging in high-profile activities, landing notable positions, and achieving big results. Following deep desires may lead to such outcomes, but not necessarily. Reducing greatness to honors, positions, riches, or similar metrics is a trap, as it leads to ego-driven ambition, radical independence, workaholism, and perfectionism. In the Spiritual Exercises, Ignatius warns us about the seduction of seeking "the empty honors of this world," a gateway to "overweening pride" (SE 142). To avoid any confusion, better to think of magnanimity as a reflection of *how* we do things more than *what* we accomplish. In an address to students at Jesuit schools in Italy and Albania, in June 2013, Pope Francis explained magnanimity in these words:

> What does being magnanimous mean? It means having a great heart, having greatness of mind; it means having great ideals, the wish to do great things to respond to what God asks of us. Hence also, for this very reason, to do well the routine things of every day and all the daily actions, tasks, meetings with people; doing the little everyday things with a great heart open to God and to others.

Looked at in this way, magnanimity is a countercultural virtue. Magnanimous people are open to any outcome, big or small, as long as they stay true to who they are and remain faithful to those they serve. Guided by their inner compass, they can accept success or failure, praise or critique, fame or derision, upward or downward mobility. They are free to love and serve, regardless of circumstance. After the fall of South Vietnam in 1975, Cardinal François-Xavier Nguyên van Thuân spent thirteen years imprisoned by the communist government, much of the time in solitary confinement. There, in an environment of many diminishments, his large heart grew even more. With inspiring inner freedom, he chose as his mission "to live the present moment, filling it to the brim with love." He lived with magnanimous conviction: "I will seize the occasions that present themselves every day; I will accomplish ordinary actions in an extraordinary way."

Every day, people do great things that we may miss because we are not seeing deeply enough. We look only for earth-shattering results or blaring trumpets, but greatness comes in different forms. A friend of mine is extraordinary in her ability to listen, never multitasking while on the phone, always looking me in the eye when in person. She reminds me of the French philosopher Simone Weil's refreshing insight that "attention is the rarest and purest form of generosity."

I once worked with someone who never called attention to himself; he did his work cheerfully and faithfully. Our office would have fallen apart without him. I also think of so many parents who without fanfare raised incredible human beings, the only important measure of success they may have ever wanted. At the conclusion of her novel *Middlemarch*, George Eliot describes the magnanimity of her central character, Dorothea, who stands in for these friends and so many other everyday saints who do ordinary things extraordinarily well:

> Her full nature . . . spent itself in channels which had no great name on the earth. But the effect of her being on those around her was incalculably diffusive: for the growing good of the world is partly dependent on unhistoric acts; and that things are not so ill with you and me as they might have been, is half owing to the number who lived faithfully a hidden life, and rest in unvisited tombs.

After my junior year of high school, I spent the summer working for the Special Olympics Summer World Games and learned an invaluable lesson about what greatness really means. The origins of Special Olympics date to the summer of 1962. Eunice Kennedy Shriver, the sister of the sitting president at the time, invited dozens of children and young adults with intellectual disabilities to her Maryland home for swimming, arts and crafts, and field events. Camp Shriver, as it was known, blossomed into an international movement to empower those with intellectual and developmental disabilities to develop their talents and grow in confidence and joy as they shared their gifts with the community. Special Olympics, formally established in 1968, today supports over five million athletes and their families in more than 170 countries.

The games I attended in high school were held at Louisiana State University in Baton Rouge. You could cut the summer's humidity with a knife, but the athletes did not care. More than the humidity, I could feel the joy, mixed with nervous anticipation as the sixth international summer games began. Hundreds of athletes gathered in the stadium and pronounced in unison the Special Olympian's oath: "Let me win. But if I cannot win, let me be brave in the attempt."

I tended to a host of logistical details to assist the coaches, athletes, and organizers, but my main job was to listen, watch, and learn. As a sixteen-year-old dealing with my own insecurities, I was initially uncomfortable relating to the athletes, many my own age. I dealt with my awkwardness by busying myself with mundane tasks I could master. Watching the competition, however, my heart opened, and I learned one of the most important lessons that Special Olympics teaches: to define people not by what they cannot do but by what they can do and how they do it—with courage and grit, with greatness. The competition was serious, but it was always marked by a palpable spirit of camaraderie and friendship as athletes helped and supported one another. Families cheered on all the athletes. I have never met so many large-hearted people in one place.

Years later, the lessons linger, and I understand more about what the Shrivers were up to. It is so easy to buy into mainstream culture's fixation on independence and power, productivity and efficiency, or a certain idea of physical prowess and beauty. Special Olympics challenges our priorities, daring us to live counterculturally by valuing community, cooperation, and other forms of human achievement and beauty. Special Olympics, and similar groups, build relationships based on mutuality, not condescension.

Eunice Kennedy Shriver died at home in 2009, surrounded by her children and many grandchildren. In her life of public service, typical of her family, she had done so much good. Her son, and my good friend, Tim recounts:

> Toward the end of her life and despite all her work, she worried that she'd done almost nothing of significance. "You should write a book," I said to her a year before she died. "I'd have nothing to write," she answered. "All I ever did was teach children with intellectual disabilities to swim." The work was never done for her, and rest never came. She kept the faith. That was enough.

To the end, Eunice Shriver's humility anchored her magnanimity. In her long, very public life, she accomplished many noteworthy things, but her greatest achievement was to teach kids to swim, and everything else flowed from that. Each in our own way, God calls us to do "great things," whether those things become widely known or not. With holy boldness, we jump into the arena, striving valiantly with a large heart open to God and others.

# SPIRITUAL EXERCISES

- Imagine Jesus saying to you, "What do you want me to do for you?" How do you respond? Be attentive to desires beneath the desires you voice.

- Reflect on the length and breadth of your life and trace a fundamental desire that evolved, transformed, or deepened over the years. From this self-examination, what do you learn about desires? Discern those desires. Where did they come from? Where did they lead you?

- Consider people who are models of magnanimity and humility, people who do great things with largeness of heart and generosity of spirit. What makes them so laudable? Which of their virtues or personal attributes do you wish to emulate? Consider not only famous people but also people whose impact is great but who get little attention, the Dorotheas from *Middlemarch* of our world who live faithfully and generously.

- When you imagine God's dream for the world, a reign of justice, peace, and love, what specifically captures your heart, garners your interest, enlivens your imagination? Is there a cause that captivates you, a problem or injustice that vexes you, a group of people whose need stirs your compassion? How might you concretely respond in a spirit of magnanimity?

# Chapter 6

# LIVING WITH COMPASSION
## The Practice of Solidarity and Kinship

*Splagchnizomai*—one of my favorite words in the Bible. It's a Greek word, the language of the New Testament. Scripture scholars translate this and related forms of the word to describe a compassionate response. It appears, for example, in the parable of the prodigal son, which we reviewed earlier. According to Luke's Gospel, "While he was still a long way off, his father caught sight of him, and was *filled with compassion*. He ran to his son, embraced him and kissed him" (15:20, emphasis mine). Similarly, before Jesus heals people, the Gospel writers often describe him as being moved with compassion or pity. For example, according to Matthew's Gospel, "When he disembarked and saw the vast crowd, his heart was moved with pity for them, and he cured their sick" (14:14).

The English translation does not capture fully what the Gospel writers are trying to convey. Part of the Greek word *splagchnizomai* refers to our internal organs, or guts. So, what the Gospel writers are really trying to say is that upon seeing people in need, Jesus was hit in the gut. This is no fainthearted response, no reaction from a distance, no pitying in the form of condescension. Jesus had a visceral reaction that moved him, physically and emotionally. The theologian M. Shawn Copeland explains, "His very bowels churn and revolt against what he sees and hears."

*Splagchnizomai* goes to the heart of who Jesus was. He felt deeply. He got close enough to notice people, to see and hear and feel their need, so much so that it hurt, and that depth of response led him to act decisively to help people. He was, in Copeland's words, "the very compassion of God among us."

Compassion is a virtue across religious traditions, and it is cherished by people who do not align with any particular religion. It is a natural human response to human need and an example of a great desire that is worthy of eliciting. In this chapter, we reflect on compassion through the lens of Ignatian spirituality, and I present the Exercises to you as a school for loving. For Ignatius, as with other Christians, Jesus is the one who models for us love in action, so much so that most of the Exercises center on Jesus' life. Ignatius's hope is that we will become more like the one we gaze upon in the Exercises, loving others as Jesus loved.

Because of the centrality of Jesus in the Exercises, there are some who insist that the Exercises are for Christians only, but I strongly believe that the Exercises can be adapted to people from all sorts of backgrounds. Admittedly, given the time in which he lived, Ignatius likely imagined offering the Exercises only to Christians. Still, deeply embedded in the Exercises is a mode of adaptability (SE 18). Ignatius counsels directors of the Exercises that God works with each person individually (SE 15), so directors are to adapt when necessary to meet a person's need, which is its own kind of compassionate response. I trust Ignatius when he writes at the beginning of the Exercises:

> It will be very profitable for the one who is to go through the Exercises to enter upon them with magnanimity and generosity toward his Creator and Lord, and to offer Him his entire will and liberty, that His Divine Majesty may dispose of him and all he possesses according to His most holy will. (SE 5)

In other words, all Ignatius asks is that people making the Exercises be open to what God wants to show them and express a sincere desire to live with greater freedom and magnanimity. What God does with such a generous soul I leave in God's hands. We do not need to settle doctrinal debates about divine revelation or the divinity and humanity of Jesus. This profound respect for the person and a tradition of adaptability also explain how Ignatian spirituality has found a home in so many cultural and religious settings across the centuries.

## Loving Unconditionally

No matter our background, getting to know Jesus in the Exercises is time well spent, for the Spiritual Exercises remain a school for loving for all. Everyone has experience of loving and being loved. In the Christian tradition, that love is the very presence of God, however we might name or struggle to name God. In the first letter of John, we hear, "God is love, and whoever remains in love remains in God and God in him" (4:16). The writer cautions Christians who profess belief but do not love: "Beloved, let us love one another, because love is of God; everyone who loves is begotten by God and knows God. Whoever is without love does not know God, for God is love" (1 John 4:7–8). Whether Christian, Jew, Muslim, or Hindu, whether a devout believer or committed humanist, when we love, we encounter Holy Mystery. In Pope Francis's words, "Whenever we encounter another person in love, we learn something new about God" (EG 272).

John's letter includes another very important Greek word, which we also find in John's Gospel and elsewhere in the New Testament. (The letters John 1–3 and the Gospel attributed to John have their origins in the same late first-century community of Christians.) In John's Gospel, Jesus says to his disciples during the Last Supper: "I give you a new commandment: love one another. As I have loved you, so you also should love one another. This is how all will know that you are my disciples, if you have love for one another" (13:34–35). Where we read the English word *love*, the writers use in the original text a version of the Greek word, *agape*. As distinguished from other familiar Greek words, like *philia* (love between friends) and *eros* (exclusive love between romantic partners), *agape* refers to a love that is completely centered on the one who is loved. *Agape* is a self-giving love, offered without condition or expectation of anything in return. It is a total gift of self.

Such love defies easy description. Love songs, romantic poems, even greeting cards try to capture this elusive mystery of human living. The Nobel laureate and American novelist John Steinbeck wrote a letter to his teenage son, Thom, that shows one expression of what agapic loving is about:

> There are several kinds of love. One is a selfish, mean, grasping, egotistical thing which uses love for self-importance. This is the ugly and crippling kind. The other is an outpouring of everything good in you—of kindness and consideration and respect—not only the social respect of manners but the greater respect which is recognition of another person as unique and valuable. The first kind can make you sick and small and weak but the second can release in you strength, and courage and goodness and even wisdom you didn't know you had.

When I am preparing couples for marriage, I remind them that in the church's understanding, they—not the officiating minister—are the ministers of the sacrament of marriage, because their love makes present to others God's agapic love, which is faithful, unconditional, and enduring. Of course, that is a very high ideal that no one can model perfectly, every day. Married couples lay down their lives for each other, in little pieces, over a lifetime. For them—for any of us—with practice, time, and God's help, we learn to love in an other-centered way so that it becomes a part of who we are, until our last breath. As Robert F. Kennedy lay dying, the victim of an assassin's bullet, he whispered into the ear of the seventeen-year-old hotel busboy, Juan Romero, who cradled his head: "Is everybody okay?"

That's what agapic love sounds like.

In the Exercises, we find no extended discourse or teaching about love. Instead, through the Exercises and its adaptations, Ignatius helps people understand what loving and being loved looks like in the context of their life. In one of the few places where Ignatius writes about love explicitly, he gets right to the point: "Love ought to manifest itself in deeds rather than in words" (SE 230). Ignatian spirituality is very practical. We cannot just talk about love: we must do something. Ignatius adds that love involves an exchange between lovers: "the lover gives and shares with the beloved what he possesses . . . and vice versa, the beloved shares with the lover" (SE 231). Mutuality is a mark of a loving relationship. This giving is made in freedom that friends and lovers enjoy, a self-offering for the good of the other that helps each become more than they could be if alone.

## Knowing, Loving, and Following Jesus

For the Christian, Jesus is God's "love walking on this earth," to use an image from a homily by the martyred Salvadoran archbishop Óscar Romero. By coming to know Jesus in the Exercises, we are schooled in how God loves so radically and how God sees so deeply. As we pray through the Exercises, Ignatius suggests that we ask repeatedly for the following grace, or gift: "Here it will be to ask for an intimate knowledge of our Lord, who has become man for me, that I may love Him more and follow Him more closely" (SE 104).

The order here is insightful and important: to know, love, follow. Ignatius understood human nature very well. We cannot really love someone unless we first know them, otherwise it is like infatuation, which can come and go. The knowing here is not just gathering facts about someone. Ignatian knowing is heartfelt knowing, which reverences the mystery of each person. The theologian and priest Michael Himes tells the story about caring for his mother after she moved to a nursing home. She struggled with dementia. For seven years, Himes visited his mother every evening, sitting with her and often feeding her dinner. A year before she died, on a particularly tough evening when she was confused, Himes asked, "Do you know who I am?" His mother paused, looking at him carefully. "I'm sorry," she replied, "I don't know that I can remember your name, but I do know that you are someone I loved very much."

Knowing and being known in a deep way creates space for love to emerge naturally. Love draws us out of ourselves to another and evaporates self-involvement. Like the fox and the little prince, we tame one another gradually; we become tied to one another by our love. When we know and love other people, we are prepared to make the next step: we walk with them, stand by them, stick with them, help them, learn from them, or in Ignatius's words, we follow them. As the fox told the little prince, we become forever responsible for the one we have tamed with our love. Love is more than just a feeling; it is a commitment. Knowing and loving another means that we remain faithful to that person. When challenges come, love does not run but goes deeper.

Recall the grace we ask for: that we may have a deeply felt knowledge of Jesus, "who has become [human] for me" (SE 104). Those words are among the most powerful in the Exercises, if we take them to heart. From its earliest centuries, the Christian Church taught that Jesus is fully human and fully divine, in all things like us but sin. As they live this mystery—or struggle with it—Christians can lapse into favoring the divine over the human, more comfortable with leaving Jesus untouched by all the physical realities and painful complications of life that we mortals have to deal with. Ignatius offers a corrective to the tendency in the Christian tradition to treat Jesus like a divine superman who wore a human suit only for show, racing his way through history to get back to heaven.

Admittedly, God becoming human in the person of Jesus—which is called the Incarnation—is one of the mysteries of faith that defies easy explanation and invites ongoing reflection. The good news is that Ignatius did not construct the Exercises as exam prep for a course in theology. Instead, through the Exercises, he lets us live the mystery of faith and develop a theology, an understanding of God, along the way. Because love always draws close, God came as close to us as God could get: becoming a human being, in the person of Jesus. Because of the Incarnation, our path to God is not running away from the complex realities of humanity but becoming more fully human, which Jesus teaches us to do.

Ignatius had a very personal encounter with his God, and he wanted us to enjoy the same intimacy. That's why the "God became human *for me*" part is so important. God wants friendship not with humanity generally, but with *me*. I admit to some hesitation when it comes to accepting this invitation. Struggling with the complexity and ambiguities of my life, I would rather keep God and other people at a distance until I figure out everything. My house is too messy, I think, for God or love to enter my life and find a home there. Fortunately, God did not wait around for our house to be in order. He got close, leaping into history and becoming a person at a particular moment (two thousand years ago), in a particular place (Palestine), with particular and very ordinary people (Mary and Joseph and their extended family).

When tempted to avoid the "for me" part, I gaze on the painting *The Annunciation* by Henry Ossawa Tanner, an African American artist with deep religious roots. The Annunciation is the event of the angel Gabriel announcing to Mary that she will give birth to Jesus, God's beloved son (Luke 1:26–38). Tanner's painting, completed in 1898, departs from traditional depictions of the event. Tanner portrays Mary as a typical Middle Eastern woman, with dark features and long black hair in customary dress, so different from the medieval and Renaissance portrayals of a very white, European woman dressed in blue. With an expression that is curious, self-assured, and peaceful, Tanner's Mary looks at a golden shaft of light, the presence of a heavenly being. She sits not in a fancy colonnade that looks like a museum but in a room with ceramics and tiles, on a bed that is messy and unmade, a blanket falling to the floor. Tanner's painting shows me that God is okay meeting us in our messy rooms and messy lives.

To help us become more comfortable with the scandalous particularity of the Incarnation, Ignatius suggests that we immerse ourselves in scenes from the Gospel through the use of our imagination—from the moment of the Annunciation, through the public life of Jesus, and concluding with his death and resurrection. For example, Ignatius invites us to imagine that we are a servant accompanying the pregnant Mary and Joseph as they make their way to Bethlehem for the birth of Jesus: "I will make myself a poor little unworthy slave, and as though present, look upon them, contemplate them, and serve them in their needs with all possible homage and reverence" (SE 114). Imagine the road from Nazareth to Bethlehem, he writes: "Consider its length, its breadth; whether level, or through valleys and over hills. Observe also the place or cave where Christ is born; whether big or little; whether high or low; and how it is arranged" (SE 112). Hear what they are saying, and observe what they are doing (SE 115, 116). We are to apply that same level of detail as we imagine the later life of Jesus, filling in the specifics: the sights, smells, tastes, and sounds of Jesus' life.

One of my favorites exercises is to imagine Jesus during the "hidden life," the years that Jesus lived with his parents in Nazareth (SE 134, 271–73) during his boyhood, adolescence, and young adulthood. This is called the "hidden life" because the Bible gives few details of this expanse of time. As a result, we have to imagine Jesus sleeping, eating, praying, laughing, crying, bathing, making friends, working with his father, getting into arguments, maybe having a crush on someone. Such details matter because any human life is full of details, and Jesus lived a human life. The Second Vatican Council beautifully captures the gritty mystery of God becoming human for me: "For by His incarnation the Son of God has united Himself in some fashion with every man. He worked with human hands, He thought with a human mind, acted by human choice and loved with a human heart."

The invitation to use one's imagination can be attractive to the person making the Exercises, even fun, like directing or acting in a movie. But there usually comes a point when we say, *Wait, how is this praying? I'm imagining stuff that's not even in the Bible. I'm making it all up. This is me, not God.* Ignatius did not invent praying with the imagination, but he did help popularize it. Ignatius trusted that God can speak to us through our imagining as much as through our thinking and remembering. Imagining is "knowing through exploration," as the Irish poet and theologian John O'Donohue proposes. Think of prayer, then, as a wonderful exploration or a free-flowing, lively kind of conversation between God and our deepest selves. We can trust that God accompanies us in our exploration and shows up when we pray (and even when we don't!). Admittedly, sometimes our imagination does get carried away. How do we know the limits? Simply ask: *Is my imagining this scene or conversation helping me grow in my relationship with God? Am I getting to know and love Jesus more? Am I coming to know and love myself and others better?* In other words, discern what's happening when you pray, paying particular attention to what you learn and feel and to where the exploration leads you.

Ultimately, the point of relying on our imagination in the Exercises is not simply to entertain, inspire, or teach an ethical lesson. The point is not admiration but transformation. Using our God-given imagination, we let ourselves be tamed or transformed by the one we come to know and love deeply. We become someone we have always been called to be. Any encounter with Jesus will not leave us the same. As we grow in heartfelt knowledge of Jesus in the Gospels, we learn his way of doing things, his way of seeing and feeling and loving deeply. We become more like the one we follow. This transformation has very practical consequences. Pope Francis asks the rhetorical question: "Do we think that Jesus' incarnation is simply a past event that has nothing to do with us personally?" He responds for us:

> Believing in Jesus means giving him our flesh with the humility and courage of Mary, so that he can continue to dwell in our midst. It means giving him our hands, to caress the little ones and the poor; our feet, to go forth and meet our brothers and sisters; our arms, to hold up the weak and to work in the Lord's vineyard; our minds, to think and act in the light of the Gospel; and especially to offer our hearts to love and to make choices in accordance with God's will.

# Learning from the Good Samaritan

In the parable of the good Samaritan (Luke 10:25–37), Jesus summarizes in story form his approach to caring for people and our duty to do the same. Jesus is prompted to share the parable by a question from a lawyer who is trying to test him. Having accurately recited the ancient law to love God and neighbor, the lawyer asks, "And who is my neighbor?" This is another way of asking, Whom am I required to love? Behind the lawyer's question is a cultural belief in Jesus' time that we have to care only for people we know or people in our ethnic or social group. Jesus disrupts this way of thinking by presenting as the main character of his parable a Samaritan. There was great enmity between Jews and Samaritans, distant cousins who shared a history but over time took very different approaches to religious practice.

The story dramatically opens: a man, presumably a Jew, is walking down the road from Jerusalem to nearby Jericho and is robbed, stripped, beaten, and left "half dead." A Jewish priest walks down the road, "but when he saw him, he passed by on the opposite side." Another religious official, a Levite, does the same. "But a Samaritan traveler who came upon him was moved with compassion at the sight. He approached the victim, poured oil and wine over his wounds and bandaged them. Then he lifted him up on his own animal, took him to an inn and cared for him. The next day he took out two silver coins and gave them to the innkeeper with the instruction, 'Take care of him. If you spend more than what I have given you, I shall repay you on my way back.'"

All three saw the beat-up man, but only one was moved with compassion. Here we again find that most important word: *splagchnizomai.* Deeply moved, hit in the gut, the Samaritan acts. He is free, while the others are filled with fear and self-preoccupations. The Samaritan gets close—very close—to the victim: tending to his wounds, bandaging them (perhaps tearing his own clothes to make the bandage?), and lifting him up. The good Samaritan involves another in his care of the injured man, the innkeeper, who exercises hospitality that was missing at the beginning of Jesus' own life when his parents found no room at the inn in Bethlehem (Luke 2:7). Here, in Jesus' telling of the parable, a community of compassion is formed. Reflecting on this link between the two inns in Luke's Gospel, Jesuit theologian Gerald O'Collins observes, "Love is a hospitality that makes everyone welcome. So often love is simply that–being a good host."

Once we see a person in need, we may be tempted to walk by or shut the door, to retreat to "those personal or communal niches which shelter us from the maelstrom of human misfortune," as Pope Francis acknowledges (EG 270). To his fellow Christians, Francis puts it plainly, "I prefer a Church which is bruised, hurting and dirty because it has been out on the streets, rather than a Church which is unhealthy from being confined and from clinging to its own security" (EG 49). In the face of such temptations, Francis urges all people of goodwill to "run the risk of a face-to-face encounter with others, with their physical presence which challenges us, with their pain and their pleas, with their joy which infects us in our close and continuous interaction" (EG 88). Whenever we enter the complex reality or chaos of another person's life and "know the power of tenderness," Francis writes, "our lives become wonderfully complicated" (EG 270). How can complication be so wonderful when it is also so time-consuming, awkward, taxing, or frustrating? Simply because it is an experience of love, which is the most wonderful thing in the world.

In his bestselling novel *The Lincoln Highway*, Amor Towles offers another lesson in the parable of the good Samaritan, through the eyes of the kind and perceptive Sister Agnes, a nun who spent her life working in an orphanage. After one of the boys returns to the orphanage at an older age to cause some well-intentioned trouble, she is understanding more than irritated, remembering the pain the boy carries. Recalling the parable of the good Samaritan, she counsels his irritated friend:

> A good Christian shows compassion toward those who are in difficulty. And that is an important part of the parable's meaning. But an equally important point that Jesus is making is that we do not always get to *choose* to whom we should show our charity.

We are moved by another's need, not their affiliation to us.

Jesus concludes the parable with a question to the lawyer, "Which of these three, in your opinion, was neighbor to the robbers' victim?"

The lawyer responds, "The one who treated him with mercy." Jesus then instructs him, "Go and do likewise." The most provocative and instructive twist in the parable is that the hero of the story told by Jesus, a Jew, is a Samaritan, not the religiously minded Jewish officials. Pope Francis observes that "those who claim to be unbelievers can sometimes put God's will into practice better than believers" (FT 74). Belief in and worship of God are not enough: faith must be put into action, in concrete acts of mercy.

## Living in Solidarity with Others

Jesus' lesson to the lawyer—and to us—calls to mind Ignatius's two statements about love: that love must show itself more by deeds than by words, and that love is a relationship of mutuality. Our duty to care for others is based not on whether we know them or whether they are part of our ethnic or social group. It is based on the reality of another human being in need, and upon seeing the need, we have a duty to act. In the tradition of Catholic social teaching, the principle of solidarity reflects this obligation. According to the principle, we are all brothers and sisters, bound together by a bond of interdependence or mutuality. Solidarity proclaims that we belong to one another, or, to use an Irish adage, we live in the shelter of one another. Made in the image of God, each person has a dignity that can never be taken away, and we have a duty to promote and protect the dignity of others, simply because they are human beings, children of God, like us. Solidarity extends particularly to those whose needs are most pressing, those who are poor, excluded, or marginalized because of who they are.

In recent years, the church's reflection on the meaning of solidarity has deepened, embracing solidarity with all of God's creation and with future generations affected by the decisions we make today. In his groundbreaking encyclical *Laudato si'*, Pope Francis writes, "As part of the universe, called into being by one Father, all of us are linked by unseen bonds and together form a kind of universal family, a sublime communion which fills us with a sacred, affectionate, and humble respect" (LS 89). Francis ties together the different strands of solidarity. Caring for one another, caring for future generations, caring for the poor and dispossessed, and caring for the earth are intertwined movements of heartfelt compassion. To separate them is to divide our heart (LS 91-92).

Moved by the need of another, we may be tempted to quickly fix problems or provide easy answers, but acting in this way might undermine an important aspect of solidarity: mutuality of relationship. Of course, we must help someone in need, but we must do so in a way that does not turn the person into an object of our generosity. Always being the helper can be an excuse to control. By creating space for others to help us and share their wisdom, we empower them. Pope Francis captures in a few words what this schooling in solidarity is about: "This is why I want a Church which is poor and for the poor. They have much to teach us. . . . We are called to find Christ in them, to lend our voice to their causes, but also to be their friends, to listen to them, to speak for them and to embrace the mysterious wisdom which God wishes to share with us through them" (EG 198).

When, during my first year as a Jesuit, I was sent to Mexico to learn Spanish and work with the Jesuits there, I lived on a hill overlooking Guadalajara, in one of the more destitute barrios of the city. The differences between my neighbors and me were so stark. As a wealthier, white, educated North American, I felt so out of place. A week or two into my stay, I was studying in a room I shared with two other younger Jesuits. I heard a commotion in the street. Looking out the window, I noticed a stream of people walking toward a house on the corner, just up the hill from the Jesuit residence. Bored with conjugating Spanish verbs, I stepped outside and joined the crowd. We entered the courtyard of a house, filled with people. At the center stood an older woman of short stature, barely visible, though she had everyone's attention. She was an *abuela*, a grandmother, a matriarch of this part of the barrio, and she was leading an Ash Wednesday service. I joined the line of people to receive ashes on the forehead, a customary ritual for the holy day.

As I stepped forward when it was my turn, she smiled, reached up, and tenderly etched a sign of the cross with the ashes on my forehead. In Spanish, she uttered the customary prayer: "Remember, man, that you are dust, and to dust you shall return." All differences vanished. I was just another human being with all the other people there, strangers at first, now my brothers and sisters, bound together in solidarity. She leveled the playing field. Sure, I was in Mexico to offer my talents and time as I could. But I was also there to receive and learn something more than just Spanish. In the weeks I was with them, she and others I met taught me how I overvalued self-sufficiency at the expense of community. With them, I came to appreciate the depth of their faith as they relied on God so completely when institutions like the government and even the church had let them down.

The *abuela* was my first teacher, but there have been so many others over my years as a Jesuit. As I have shared previously in this book, the men in the detention center revealed to me a vocation within a vocation. The Special Olympians taught me not to be captive to appearance and to see beauty and valor in unexpected places. For two summers during my formation as a Jesuit, I worked at a camp in the Blue Ridge Mountains that hosted families mostly from the inner cities of Philadelphia, Baltimore, and Washington. The weeklong program was a blend of typical camp activities (swimming, sports, campfires), religious activities, and lots of eating! The purpose was to help families draw closer together, mend any hurts, and deepen their faith. Our staff did lots of serving—the days were long—but as the week went on, we were invited into the lives of the families, who came from very different backgrounds than most of us. Those differences did not matter. On that mountain, we were just a bunch of people who were having fun together and talking about stuff that really mattered to all of us.

The Jesuit Greg Boyle knows the transformative power of solidarity steeped in mutuality. In 1986, he became pastor of Dolores Mission Church in East Los Angeles, situated in an area with the highest concentration of gang activity and the largest public housing projects in the city. Seeing people in need, Boyle and his partners devised a new way to care for those who had been previously incarcerated and involved in gangs: provide jobs and job training to reduce recidivism, restore broken relationships, and offer hope. Homeboy Industries was founded in 1988 and over the years developed a host of social enterprises, including catering and food service, silk-screening, and electronics recycling. Today, Homeboy is the largest gang intervention, rehab, and reentry program in the world. To characterize the organization's mission, Boyle speaks of kinship, "not serving the other, but being one with the other." Kinship is solidarity up close. In his bestselling book *Tattoos on the Heart,* Boyle quotes with appreciation Sister Elaine Roulet, a kindred spirit, who innovated a number of programs for mothers who were incarcerated in the New York City area. When asked, "How do you work with the poor?" she answered simply: "You don't. You share your life with the poor."

Being with, walking with, standing with, sharing with—the *with* signals a relationship of solidarity and kinship. Sharing our life with others as Jesus did. Recall in the Exercises the call of Jesus to build God's reign of justice, peace, and love (SE 95). Ignatius portrays Jesus as saying "labor with me" as together we advance God's reign, an astounding invitation to friendship and partnership for mission. Jesus does not issue orders from above; he accompanies us, a companion on the journey.

I remember a journey I took with students on the Arizona-Mexico border. The sun baked us as we walked through the desert. The path was barely visible through the brush, but the markers were clearly evident: a discarded plastic water bottle, a dirt-covered bag, a piece of colorful clothing caught on cactus—all signs of migrants from Mexico and Central America who had crossed this part of the desert. Our guide was Peter Neeley, a charismatic Jesuit in a big straw hat that covered his fair Irish skin (and the same Jesuit who orientated me to the immigration detention center in Los Angeles a few years earlier). The desert terrain, so wide and open, is fraught with danger, he pointed out. The risk of dehydration and sunstroke during the day yields to the risk of exposure to the bitter cold at night. Crossing at night can help migrants escape the notice of border patrol, but the darkness makes it easy to stumble onto snakes and into deep ravines. Thousands try to cross each year; hundreds die on the journey. Some are exploited and abused by *coyotes,* the people paid to guide them through the desert. Many give up and turn themselves in to border patrol. A fortunate few make it without detection.

Our walk lasted only an hour or two. I saw on the students' young faces that they got the message. We returned to the *comedor* run by the Kino Border Initiative, a cross-border organization dedicated to accompanying, serving, and advocating for migrants. The *comedor* sits on the border in Nogales, a city divided by concrete barriers and a steel-slated wall: Mexico on one side, the United States on the other. Every day, the sisters, Jesuits, and volunteers fed migrants, who were either preparing to cross the border or had recently been deported. A provocative mural of Leonardo da Vinci's *The Last Supper* was painted on the cinderblock wall in vivid colors: Jesus and the disciples are dark skinned, dressed like migrants, and eating the food typical of migrants. In the *comedor*, we served simple but hearty meals, but the sisters reminded us of the more important work of sitting with the migrants, regardless of how well we knew Spanish. Listen and learn first, then respond to the need they express, not to the need you presume they have. Witness their faith, the sisters counseled. When so many have let them down, and lacking power and privilege, they know that God is their strength, the source of their resilience.

After the midday lunch, we visited a shelter for women and children across the street, in a nondescript, multistory apartment building. The women there told us stories of gang violence that drove them to flee their home countries, and they recounted the abuse they suffered on the journey north. They were safe, at least for the time being. A young woman from our group, a Mexican American first-year student, translated for us through tears.

One student in our group, Chris, returned the next summer to live and work with an organization called No More Deaths, delivering water, clothing, blankets, and medical aid to migrants in distress in the desert through which we briefly trekked. Accompany first, then serve. Another student, Joanna, returned to the border after graduation and has worked there for years with the Kino Border Initiative. Accompany first, then advocate. Over the years, I have returned to the border with students and on my own. I keep learning.

# Creating Communities of Kinship

Solidarity does not just describe interpersonal relationships; it is a principle of organization for societies and social groups. Our compassionate response can take two forms: one of charity and the other of justice. Charity refers to individual acts of compassion. It is a personal response, like the Samaritan's, to someone in need. *Charity* is a word of Latin origin that is synonymous with *agape:* unconditional, other-centered loving. Justice expands the scope of our compassionate response. We address systemic issues and social structures that are root causes of individual need or harm. The theologian Jon Sobrino, SJ, writing from his experience in El Salvador, describes justice as "the name love acquires when it comes to entire majorities of people unjustly oppressed." Ideally, charity and justice go hand in hand; we need both to make real God's dream for the world. In his reflection on the parable of the good Samaritan, Pope Francis puts the challenge plainly: "The decision to include or exclude those lying wounded along the roadside can serve as a criterion for judging every economic, political, social, and religious project. Each day we have to decide whether to be Good Samaritans or indifferent bystanders" (FT 69).

In a sermon in Memphis on the night before he was assassinated, Rev. Dr. Martin Luther King Jr. reflected on the parable and offered insight into the distinction between charity and justice. Praising the selflessness of the Samaritan, King noted the primary difference between the Samaritan and the religious officials: "The first question that the priest asked—the first question that the Levite asked was, 'If I stop to help this man, what will happen to me?' But then the Good Samaritan came by. And he reversed the question: 'If I do not stop to help this man, what will happen to him?'" This inversion of perspective is part of what Pope Francis has called the "revolution of tenderness" (EG 88), a phrase that carries with it notions of both charity (tenderness) and justice (revolution).

King's sermon takes a provocative turn when he raises questions that Jesus did not raise in the parable's telling. King reflects on the motivations of the priest and the Levite in not helping the Samaritan. Maybe they did not want to become ritually impure by touching the injured man, which would have prevented them from serving in the temple. Maybe they were afraid of getting beat up themselves. Perhaps the robbers were still around, or the man on the side of the road was part of the setup to lure them. Or maybe, King wonders, they were on their way to organize a Jericho Road Improvement Association, which is an allusion to the Montgomery Improvement Association that managed the successful bus boycott after Rosa Parks's act of protest there. King mused to the crowd in Memphis, "That's a possibility. Maybe they felt that it was better to deal with the problem from the causal root, rather than to get bogged down with an individual effect." With King's inspiration, we can imagine the association addressing questions like: Why was the road so dangerous in the first place? How can we make it safer so that no one else gets hurt? How can we remedy the historical sources of conflict between Jews and Samaritans?

A Jericho Road Improvement Association would be a justice response to the injured man's need, but importantly it would be inadequate, even callous, without a charitable response as well. We do not want to leave the injured man bleeding to death while we write the bylaws for our new Association.

Father Boyle integrates the two levels of compassionate response with the image of a circle of compassion: "We imagine no one standing outside of that circle, moving ourselves closer to the margins so that the margins themselves will be erased." It is not about going to the margins and bringing people back to the center, which the privileged and powerful have constructed. Justice is about creating a new center, or a new community of kinship. "At the edges, we join the easily despised and the readily left out. We stand with the demonized so that the demonizing will stop. We situate ourselves right next to the disposable so that day will come when we stop throwing people away." In the circle of compassion, with no daylight between us, we who are moved with compassion to help are changed too. Boyle writes from his experience, "We are sent to the margins not to make a difference but so that the folks on the margins will make *us* different."

Making this move to the margins, enlarging the circle of compassion, and creating a new center from the standpoint of the powerless is hard work. It costs us in various ways. It takes time, so we need to summon patience. It takes humility because we no longer control from our center, and we are likely to face setbacks along the way. Redrawing the lines of relationship may cost us friends and reputation. Being with people different from us and standing in unfamiliar places may be uncomfortable at first. Getting "hit in the gut" and allowing ourselves to be vulnerable is no fun. Hearts that are open can break. Love that is given to another can be rejected.

Such costs can be so painful that we are understandably tempted to retreat to our "personal and communal niches," as Pope Francis put it. This retreat, however, costs us in different ways. Instead of building a culture of encounter, we create a culture of indifference, as Pope Francis calls it, through our intentional moral blindness. What we see depends on where we stand. If we remove ourselves from the circle of compassion, we will not see the person who needs us or the injustice begging to be addressed. The hurt only continues; the injustice persists.

Not seeing need or walking by need that we do see may spare us from feeling conflicted or uncomfortable, but the cost to us only multiplies. Instead of breaking, our heart becomes hardened. We become less human. In his classic book *The Four Loves*, the theologian C. S. Lewis wrote:

> To love at all is to be vulnerable. Love anything, and your heart will certainly be wrung and possibly be broken. If you want to make sure of keeping it intact, you must give your heart to no one. . . . Wrap it carefully round with hobbies and little luxuries; avoid all entanglements; lock it up safe in the casket or coffin of your selfishness. But in that casket—safe, dark, motionless, airless—it will change. It will not be broken; it will become unbreakable, impenetrable, irredeemable.

With all its worthwhile risks, loving so radically is a courageous act.

Even with the costs, the good news is that the circle of compassion is liberating for everyone. Those in need are helped, injustices are rectified, and the illusion of separateness among us is shattered. We meet new friends.

We love and are loved in surprising ways. We find healing and help that we did not know we needed. And for the Christian, in the circle of compassion we find Jesus. While Jesus did not hesitate to engage with the elite of his time, he spent most of his days exactly where Boyle directs us: at the margins, with people excluded and considered outcasts in his culture. Boyle writes, "The strategy of Jesus is not centered in taking the right stand on issues, but rather in standing in the right place—with the outcast and those relegated to the margins."

In the end, our discomfort may be a sign that we are responding to the counterculturral call to live God's reign of justice, peace, and love and to follow Jesus, who both consoled and unsettled people. Óscar Romero led the Catholic Church in El Salvador amid civil war during the 1970s. Though timid at first, he gradually found his voice after listening to and walking with the poor of his country and with the victims of war. The more he saw, the more he spoke out. In a pastoral letter, Romero called for a church in El Salvador that lives and serves among those who are poor, "in solidarity with them, running the risks they run, enduring the persecution that is their fate, ready to give the greatest possible testimony to its love by defending and promoting those who were first in Jesus' love."

Romero stood in the right place, but it cost him. His challenge to oppressive political and military leaders led to repeated harassment and ultimately his assassination, while he was celebrating Mass in 1980. As the civil war escalated, Archbishop Romero said, "A church that doesn't provoke any crises, a Gospel that doesn't unsettle, a word of God that doesn't get under anyone's skin, a word of God that doesn't touch the real sin of the society in which it is being proclaimed—what gospel is that?" Even with the risks of living in solidarity, we embrace doing so realistically and hopefully as an expression of agapic loving and justice making.

## Practicing Compassion

We must practice compassion if it is to become part of who we are, if it is to become our default setting, so to speak, in how we approach any situation.

This training is how we tie ourselves to one another or tame one another as we build friendships based in solidarity. Fortunately, life gives us lots of opportunities to practice compassion. But there's a real temptation to generalize, and not be practical. It is easy to love humanity generally, but loving a particular person in front of me is much more challenging, given the complexity and ambiguity of any human life. A young man wrote to the Catholic activist Dorothy Day asking for advice because he was struggling with his parents. Her reply was quite down-to-earth: "When you say you want to love your fellow men you just have to begin at home. . . . It is so easy to love people at a distance—not folks at home. I know how it is. We each of us have been thru it all."

Taking a cue from Ignatius's principle that love ought to show itself more by deeds than by words, I close this chapter by offering some practical suggestions on practicing compassion.

**First, when given a choice, "err in the direction of kindness,"** as the award-winning author George Saunders counsels. In an address at Syracuse University in 2013, Saunders recounted the story of a girl in his seventh-grade class who was teased by other students and mostly kept to herself. Decades later, Saunders still regrets not doing more to help her: "What I regret most in my life are *failures of kindness*. Those moments when another human being was there, in front of me, suffering, and I responded . . . sensibly. Reservedly. Mildly." Saunders acknowledged that with age and experience, acting kindly becomes easier, but he encouraged the students to practice kindness now. "Who, in *your* life, do you remember most fondly, with the most undeniable feelings of warmth? Those who were kindest to you, I bet."

**Second, apply the Presupposition of the *Spiritual Exercises*.** At the beginning of the *Exercises*, Ignatius offers some practical advice: when talking with someone, presume the goodwill of the other, and try to put a positive interpretation on what they are saying. If you cannot, then correct them in truth and "with all kindness" (SE 22). Applying the Presupposition is especially helpful when dealing with people who "push your buttons" or drive you crazy, when it's really tempting to make snap judgments or dismiss the other. The Presupposition can also open for us a path to forgiveness. It asks us to step back and change perspective, to replace judgment with wonder: *What's going on in them? What are they trying to say or do? How does God view them?* Fr. Boyle writes, "The ultimate measure of health in any community might well reside in our ability to stand in awe at what folks have to carry rather than in judgment at how they carry it." One of Boyle's "homies" remarked, "When I'm talking with someone I just don't like, I remind myself, this guy's mother loves him. It softens me into a corner."

**Third, exercise self-compassion.** Stop beating yourself up (which, by the way, is an awful image when you think about it). If we are more compassionate with ourselves, we are likely to be more compassionate with others. Like every other human being, we are beautifully limited. We are sinners loved unconditionally by God, as the Exercises reveal to us. Such mercy is not carte blanche to do whatever we want, but a source of goodness: having been loved or forgiven in such a profound way, we are inspired to be better people—not perfect, just better. In fact, embracing our imperfection creates space for others to enter our lives. In the first (and best) Rocky film, the streetwise Rocky Balboa explained his relationship with his girlfriend, Adrian: "She's got gaps, I've got gaps, together we fill gaps." In another example, in his classic song, "Anthem," the Canadian songwriter and poet Leonard Cohen views imperfection hopefully, claiming that, although there's a crack in everything, "that's how the light gets in."

**Finally, maintain healthy humility, expressed with a good sense of humor and an ability to laugh at yourself.** Breaking news: we all have foibles and idiosyncrasies that drive other people crazy! We have hurt people without intending it. When I was a Jesuit novice, I served in a parish in Syracuse with a very diverse community. It was known as one of the most welcoming and inclusive parishes in the diocese. For years, they had a large banner hanging on the front of the old church, just above the main entrance: "Sinners Welcome." Such honest recognition levels the playing field and is a form of kinship: we are all beautifully flawed children of God, and we all need healing. Pema Chödrön writes, "Maybe the most important teaching is to lighten up and relax. It's such a huge help in working with our crazy mixed-up minds to remember that what we're doing is unlocking a softness that is in us and letting it spread. We're letting it blur the sharp corners of self-criticism and complaint."

Living with compassion means less judgment and more tenderness. Instead of condemnation, we offer words of grateful admiration. Rather than looking at everyone with a critical eye, we see with the heart. When Michelangelo received the commission to sculpt the biblical hero David, he was given a slab of marble a prior artist had rejected for its poor quality. It lay unfinished for more than two decades. Some saw it as ruined, imperfect. Michelangelo saw something very different. With a master artist's penetrating gaze, something beautiful was revealed to him. That's how God looks upon us, seeing what is beautiful and possible even in our imperfections, embracing what others reject, unlocking tenderness in us and letting it spread.

## SPIRITUAL EXERCISES

- Consider the parable of the good Samaritan. When have you acted like the good Samaritan? Like the religious officials who walked by? Like the man in need of healing? Recall specific examples of people showing kindness to you and you showing kindness to others. Where is there room for more kindness or tenderness in your life?

- Read Matthew 14:13–21 or Matthew 20:29–34 and put yourself into the action of the Gospel scene. Imagine the sights, sounds, and people in the scene. Go through it once as if observing the action, and then review the scene again, putting yourself in the story somewhere. Imagine Jesus being moved with compassion. What does Jesus look like? What does he say and do? How do people respond? Imagine that you tell Jesus something you need. How does he look upon you? What does he say to you?

- Remember a time when you responded compassionately to a person in need. What were you feeling? How did the other person respond? What did you learn? Was there mutuality of relationship present? What justice questions does this interaction raise?

- Because what we see depends on where we stand, assess where and with whom you usually stand. Do you allow yourself to be in unfamiliar settings, with people different from you? Do you tend to retreat to familiar and comfortable niches? When you are in public settings, are you attentive to what and who is around you, or do you tend to look down at a screen in your hand or get easily distracted? Another way of standing in different places is learning about issues and needs that you ordinarily do not consider for lack of interest or understanding. How might you expand your scope of learning?

- Is there someone in your life with whom you need to exercise Ignatius's Presupposition? What is the other person trying to say? What is that person's intention? How might you correct the person in truth and love, if necessary? Where might you be called to forgive someone or accept forgiveness of another?

# Chapter 7

# LIVING IN HOPE
## Finding Meaning in Suffering and Loss

My parents moved our family to South Florida in 1970. They had both grown up in Montreal, the city where my siblings, Cathy and Andy, and I were born. It was a big change for them, especially raising three very young children far from their family and friends up north. But it was also an adventure (and a gift for our relatives who visited regularly in the winter). Not long after getting settled, my dad bought a convertible, built a pool in our backyard, and planted fruit trees around the house: orange, grapefruit, and lime.

My father died from complications of Parkinson's disease in his eighties. We were grateful that the disease progressed slowly, but ultimately it took away his ability to swallow. A month before he died, he was able to sit at the dinner table at Thanksgiving but could not manage to eat the turkey and mashed potatoes we prepared. He kept eyeing the key lime pie, his favorite dessert, made with the limes that came from our yard (and that also got good use in my mother's gin and sodas). Pushing the uneaten main course aside, I scooped a spoonful of the key lime pie with a dab of whipped cream and fed him, which he managed to get down, with a smile. It was the last solid food my father would eat.

While my dad enjoyed his convertible and pool, my mom started playing lots of golf. She loved playing and quickly became the best player in the family. In her fifties she scored a hole in one, a rarity in the game. A poster marking the event hung in our home for years. My mom watched a lot of golf on the weekends, rooting for her favorite players. She stopped playing in her mid-seventies, when she lost strength and energy, a symptom of the congestive heart failure she suffered. On one of my last visits before she died in her eighties, I sat next to her hospital bed, watching a golf tournament with her. She drifted in and out of sleep and missed a hole in one. I looked over to her with excitement, but her eyes were closed. I didn't wake her.

The lime tree died not long after, the last of those original fruit trees to survive hurricanes and blight.

Cathy, Andy, and I were able to arrange hospice care for both our parents in the home we had moved into in 1970. At my father's bedside, I sat with him at night and said my prayers out loud, prayers he taught me as a child. Though seemingly not conscious, his lips moved slightly as I prayed the Our Father and Hail Mary with him. One of the last things my mother whispered to me was, "Are you happy?" This was a frequent question from her. I assured her I was, and that Cathy and Andy were doing great. She smiled and drifted back to sleep.

My parents died a decade apart in familiar, comfortable surroundings, with the help of devoted hospice care staff. The ritual of dying was made a little easier for me because, years before as a young Jesuit, I had worked as an orderly for a summer at a palliative care hospital for adults with advanced cancer and other life-limiting illnesses. I was blessed with an amazing person as my nurse supervisor, Rhona, who over the years had broken in many other squeamish Jesuits with skill, generosity, and a lot of patience. As I sat at my parents' bedside, memories of the people I met that summer came back to me, as did the lessons that Rhona taught me, well beyond the logistics of patient care. Whether patients were conscious or not, she always talked to them ("You never know what they can hear" was her refrain). Rhona never pretended that the patients were not dying. With her graceful presence, she honored where each patient and their family was on the journey we all eventually make between life and death and life after death. I heard Rhona's voice echo in my words as I whispered to my father: "It's okay. You can let go. We are here. We love you. You are surrounded by love."

As anyone who has lost a loved one knows well, grief has its own rhythm. After my parents died, grief came and went like ocean waves on the beach near our Florida home: washing over me, then receding, at various intervals depending on the currents of a day's routine. The Irish poet and theologian John O'Donohue gets it right:

> There are days when you wake up happy;
> Again inside the fullness of life,
> Until the moment breaks
> And you are thrown back
> Onto the black tide of loss.
>
> Days when you have your heart back,
> You are able to function well
> Until in the middle of work or encounter,
> Suddenly with no warning,
> You are ambushed by grief.

—"For Grief"

In our loss, my siblings and I were gentle with one another, each allowing the others to grieve in their own way. The rituals of the Catholic funerals were comforting in their familiarity. The music, prayers, and liturgical actions all proclaimed in different ways the heart of Christian theology: in death, life is changed, not ended.

While embracing the uniqueness of my journey of grieving, I was also pretty good at avoiding the pain of deep loss. At my parents' funerals, I played the priest more than the son. I quickly returned to work and stayed busy. But grief caught up to me, as it does. A few months after my father died, I started to cry while watching a baseball game, a sport he had loved and that I resisted when I was younger, during an extended teenage rebellion. As she got older, my mother asked me to call her whenever I got home from my frequent business trips, even though we lived far away from each other. With some annoyance, I complied with her request. A month after she died, upon returning from a trip, I picked up my phone to call her, only to hang up in tears when I realized that she was no longer there, caring that I had returned home safely.

The waves of grief are less frequent now. Still, I miss them.

While writing this book, I watched the Disney streaming series *WandaVision*, part of the Marvel Comics universe of characters. The show, it turns out, is an extended meditation on grief. Wanda is a human who developed various superpowers, including telekinesis and mind control. Vision is an android with superior intelligence and other superpowers. Though not human in origin, he evolves and discovers more of his latent humanity, including developing an unlikely romantic relationship with Wanda. Both are part of the storied Avengers, a group of superheroes who have saved the world numerous times. Wanda does not do a very good job dealing with loss, causing a lot of unintended harm along the way. In a flashback during the eighth episode, Vision tries to console Wanda, who is mourning the death of her twin brother, as she will later mourn Vision:

*Wanda:* It's just like this wave washing over me again and again. It knocks me down and when I try to stand up, it just comes for me again. And I can't . . . It's gonna drown me.

*Vision:* No. No, Wanda.

*Wanda:* How do you know?

*Vision:* Because it can't be all sorrow, can it? I've always been alone so I don't feel the lack. It's all I've ever known. I've never experienced loss because I've never had a loved one to lose. What is grief, if not love persevering?

*Grief as love persevering* captures the complexity of our experience of loss; the reason we hurt so much is that we loved so much and let ourselves be loved. Our suffering is often coupled with some form of consolation: love that lingers, memories that soothe, a search for meaning that satisfies, or hope that comforts. All is not lost.

Earlier in the book, we discussed finding God in the beauty of nature and other people and in the ordinary moments of every day. Finding God in pain and suffering is a lot harder. Yet if we are serious about not restricting divine laboring to any one domain of our experience—if we can find

God in *all* things, even difficult things—then we face the challenge of finding meaning and hope in the midst of suffering. This is our focus in the pages that follow.

In the Christian imagination, Good Friday and Easter—suffering and hope—cannot be understood apart from each other. St. Ignatius makes the same connection in his Spiritual Exercises, where we walk with Jesus in his suffering and death as portrayed in the Gospels and follow him in his resurrected life. Whether we interpret our life with the help of these religious sources or not, each of us has lived experiences of suffering and loss and of searching for meaning and finding hope. The questions that arise from these utterly human experiences are not just academic: they hit very close to home. We thus need to be gentle with ourselves as our conversation here deepens, as we grapple with the mystery of suffering and hope, and as we encounter again the God who is Holy Mystery.

# Wrestling with the Mystery of Suffering

At the heart of this mystery is this question: If God is good and all-powerful, why does God allow suffering? Among the many questions we live and wrestle with, this is a central one. Across the centuries, theologians and philosophers have proposed a variety of answers as they consider this question. The most common response is free will: God gives us the ability to choose good and evil, and when we choose evil, we cause suffering. As for suffering caused by natural disasters, these thinkers lean on creation in a different way. God created the world with certain rules or natural laws, which make possible scientific discovery and human progress. Hurricanes and cancer cells, which can cause harm, are just following the rules of the world that God set up. For God to interfere with our free will would turn us into puppets or playthings. For God to interfere with the laws of nature would mean that we could not rely on these laws to govern our lives. Intervening to prevent harm in these ways, God might seem "nicer" but would also become more controlling, depriving us of the agency and autonomy that define a human life and make it meaningful.

These and other academic arguments to explain suffering may make sense, but they rarely satisfy, because we still suffer, which is a deeply personal experience that cuts to our core. The mind may get it, but our body still hurts and our heart still breaks. Throughout the Bible, we find people grappling with the reality of suffering amid common human struggles. They, too, try to make sense of it and reconcile their pain with their evolving understanding of God. One answer that emerges in the Old Testament, in which the law is so central to the identity of the Jewish people, is that if they follow God's commandments, they will be rewarded, and if they violate the law, then they will be punished. In this view, if people are suffering, then they must have done something to deserve it. The law of retribution, as this belief system is called, is an easy-to-apply formulation, but life, we know, is not so neat. The law of retribution does not account for the innocent who suffer, and it turns God into a vindictive or dispassionate judge.

Nowhere is the law of retribution most directly and eloquently challenged than in the book of Job, a captivating piece of literature in the Old Testament. The book was likely written during a time of great suffering for the Jewish people; their temple and holy city Jerusalem were destroyed, and many were forced into exile. While the story is not historical, the book conveys the collective wisdom of a people trying to make sense of their suffering and reconcile it with their long-held religious convictions.

The book opens with a presentation of Job's piety: he is a good and faithful man and enjoys the blessings of a large family and many possessions. The law of retribution works so far: a good person is rewarded. But that assumption is challenged in a dramatic exchange between God and Satan. God is so proud of Job, but Satan sees an opening and presents a challenge: *Of course, Job is faithful when everything goes so well for him, but will he remain so when he loses everything he loves?* God takes the wager, and poor Job begins to suffer greatly: his children die, he loses his possessions, and he is afflicted with boils all over his body. His friends show up and initially console him, but then they start to torment him. Relying on the law of retribution, they insist that Job must have done something to deserve his suffering. God is disciplining Job or sending him a wake-up call to live a better life.

In response, Job insists on his innocence, and as the story progresses, he complains more and more about his situation. He boldly and directly challenges God to give the reasons for his suffering, as if putting God on trial for causing Job's suffering. Amid all Job's laments and the back-and-forth with Job's friends, God is silent. Only at the end of the book does God speak. God does not give Job any direct answers. Instead, in an extended monologue, God reminds Job that God—not Job—is the creator of the universe and that God's ways are sometimes beyond our understanding. Out of the storm or whirlwind, God asks, "Where were you when I founded the earth? Tell me, if you have understanding" (38:4). God then describes the wonders and mysteries of all created things, both small and large.

The book concludes with Job humbled: "I have spoken but did not understand; things too marvelous for me, which I did not know. . . . I disown what I have said, and repent in dust and ashes" (42:3, 6). God restores Job's fortune, even more than he had before. He is blessed with more children and lives to old age.

The book's introduction and conclusion have always unnerved me. The image of God wagering with Satan, treating Job like a plaything, is hardly the God I want to pray to. And the book's happy ending too easily glosses over the losses Job suffered, particularly the deaths of his children. Coping with such gut-wrenching losses and pain is much harder than simply "moving on" as the book presents.

Still, the book of Job teaches us valuable lessons as we encounter suffering and loss. The author does not really answer the question about why good people suffer, an open-ended approach I like. The book refuses to give easy answers to a question that defies easy solution, as the law of retribution tried to do. Life—any of our lives—is far too complicated for that.

Job also gives me permission to cry out when I suffer. In this way, Job is consistent with other parts of the Old Testament, particularly the psalms and books about Israel's prophets, where we find heartrending laments and brutally honest pleas to God from people who are suffering. What Job asks for is that God hear his complaint and then talk with him. And this is just what God does in the book. Job laments, God listens, and then God basically responds: *I heard your cry; you are not alone; your suffering is part of something bigger that you cannot now understand.* God shows up.

Lament is a way we live the questions in a visceral, deeply personal way. The tradition of lament teaches us that prayer—our conversation with God—should not avoid what's actually going on in our lives and that God wants to hear about it, even the hard parts. God can take our complaints and does not run away or punish us for insubordination. Such honesty makes our relationship with God and others real. Instead of giving a definitive answer, God gives Job (and us) God's presence. And we learn that even if we cannot change the circumstances of our loss, we can change how we respond to that loss.

As much as we may rant and rave like Job, at some point we need to fall silent before the mystery of suffering and the mystery of God. We do not have all the answers. The drama of my suffering is part of something bigger. I do not mean that we should "suffer in silence." To the contrary, we need to let other people and God into our lives at such times, and lament is a healthy response. Yet silence also offers a way through our suffering, a gateway to deeper understanding and even hope. In the stillness, we might hear the word of God, or another, who assures us: "You are not alone. I am here." Resilience may begin to stir. Memories are given space to emerge. Love perseveres.

# Finding Meaning in Suffering

For Christians, the most eloquent response to questions about human suffering is the life, death, and resurrection of Jesus Christ. As we discussed in the previous chapter, the Gospels describe how Jesus is deeply moved (hit in the gut!) when he encounters the suffering of another. In response, Jesus heals a number of people, sometimes through a spoken word, other times through physical touch. As news spreads about his healing power, more and more people track him down and beg for help. He is attentive not just to their physical pain but also to suffering that comes from mental anguish and social isolation.

The bedrock of Christian theology is that Jesus was fully divine and fully human, like us in all things but sin. We need to take Jesus' humanity seriously. As divine, Jesus healed people, but his humanity also has something to teach us about suffering. One of the reasons he was so compassionate to others, I think, is that he knew suffering firsthand. Relying on our imagination, we can picture how Jesus might have dealt with the ordinary pains of human life as he grew up, such as suffering from illness or injury, missing his parents, mourning his father, maybe even dealing with a broken heart.

In his public ministry, the Gospels provide some specific examples of Jesus' suffering. Upon the death of his friend Lazarus, he weeps (John 11:35). He weeps again as he approaches Jerusalem near the time of his arrest (Luke 19:41). We encounter Jesus' emotional and physical distress most clearly and poignantly in the Passion, which refers to the events of his suffering and death. Jesus experiences intense emotional anguish as he is betrayed by his closest disciples and humiliated by his enemies. In the garden, with his arrest imminent, Luke's Gospel offers this detail: "He was in such agony and he prayed so fervently that his sweat became like drops of blood falling on the ground" (22:44). Each of the four Gospels details Jesus' torture and execution on the cross. In Mark's Gospel, the starkest of all the Gospels, Jesus' last words on the cross are tragically desperate, "My God, my God, why have you forsaken me?" (15:34).

We may want to explain away these harsh realities: "Jesus was divine so he didn't really feel it," or "He just went through the motions of Good Friday so he could get to Easter." In the Spiritual Exercises, Ignatius asks us to resist such thinking as we pray through the Passion: "Consider how the divinity hides itself," leaving "the most sacred humanity to suffer so cruelly" (196). As hard as it is, we should not skip over the Passion; it reveals to us something about Jesus' mind and heart, which is the mind and heart of God.

Jesus did not seek the cross but accepted it as the result of his being faithful to the mission God gave him: to build God's reign of justice, peace, and love. This reign was a threat to fear-filled, power-obsessed religious and political leaders, so they plotted to kill Jesus, to get rid of the problem. Jesus could have run, but he did not because he loved us, and love does not run. Jesus knew his purpose, and he stuck by it. He wanted so desperately to end the cycle of violence and death by taking it on directly. Love is a great feeling, but it is also a commitment, and love can cost us, sometimes dearly, as we give ourselves to another. Reflecting on the meaning of the Passion from the context of his decades living in El Salvador, the Jesuit theologian Jon Sobrino wrote, "In the cross there is great love, and love always creates hope." Christians thus dare to call such a horrible day Good Friday and wear crosses around their necks because the Passion of Jesus is a story of love and faithfulness to the end. And both point to Easter Sunday, when God's faithfulness to Jesus is gloriously revealed in the resurrection, when life vanquishes death, love conquers hate, and hope dispels fear.

Is there a meaning to Jesus' suffering, beyond serving as a gateway to the good news of Easter? An early Christian community responded to this question in a way that is helpful for us today who seek meaning in our own suffering. In the letter to the Hebrews, written to offer encouragement to a community struggling with their faith, the author presents Jesus, now in his gloried life, as one who understands people's struggles: "Because he himself was tested through what he suffered, he is able to help those who are being tested" (2:18). The writer offers this prayer: "For we do not have a high priest who is unable to sympathize with our weaknesses, but one who has similarly been tested in every way, yet without sin. So let us confidently approach the throne of grace to receive mercy and to find grace for timely help" (4:15–16). In this way, Jesus' suffering becomes a gateway to intimacy with a God who comes so close to us that God gets caught up in the violence and death-dealing of our world.

Such friendship with the Divine is empowering. Reflecting on the faith of enslaved people in the United States, the theologian M. Shawn Copeland writes, "The enslaved people's embrace of the crucified Lord was no act of self-abnegation but an act of signifying resistance." They identified with Jesus not simply because he chose to be with and serve the poor and oppressed, but because he himself was beaten, tortured, and murdered. Copeland continues, "They believed that he was one with them in their otherness and affliction, that he would help them to negotiate this world with righteous anger and dignity."

In his life, death, and resurrection, Jesus does not promise to take away our suffering, but he does promise to be with us when we suffer, which can be a source of strength and hope for us. This "being with" or accompaniment is a powerful response to another's suffering. In the Spiritual Exercises, Ignatius schools us in this kind of solidarity when he asks us to pray "for sorrow with Christ in sorrow, anguish with Christ in anguish, tears and deep grief because of the great affliction Christ endures for me" (SE 203). Just be with him, Ignatius tells us. I can tie my mind in knots, wrestling with questions about why God allows such pain in our world. I find some peace only when I summon the courage to face suffering directly so that I can be with others in their pain and perhaps do something to alleviate it.

When we are with others in their suffering, it is tempting to give answers to make ourselves feel better or feel less uncomfortable. More than answers, people in suffering want our company. When he was sixteen years old, my cousin Alex died in an avalanche while skiing with six of his classmates near Vancouver, Canada. I flew out to Calgary to be with the Canadian branch of my family. The entire city was mourning. Alex was such a lively, smart, sensitive kid. Gathered as a family, we felt his absence dearly. Alex's funeral was the last of seven. Preaching at the memorial service, I looked out on the congregation—especially his parents—who by that point were numb with the successive rituals of grieving. The words I had so carefully prepared at the time seemed inadequate. Speaking instead from the heart, I spoke of Christian hope amid profound loss and unexpected tragedy and voiced the "why" questions we were all asking. Our shared lament carried us through a difficult time, if only to the next day. Presence, I learned, is more important than eloquence, company more satisfying than answers. Maybe such accompaniment is the best answer we can give this side of heaven to the problem of suffering because it states so clearly and simply: "You are not alone. I am with you," which is what Jesus' life was all about.

# Not Rushing Easter

Whether experienced after the death of a loved one or because of another loss, our suffering usually includes some form of loneliness or emptiness. Some years ago, I left a ministry I loved, and experienced a deep loneliness in the months of transition. Surely the loneliness was tied to the sadness of leaving friends I'd grown close to, but it was more than that. There was a stripping away of identity: a familiar role, a record of accomplishment, a comfortable routine—all those things we can rely on too heavily for a sense of self-worth. For me, this time in my life was a "Holy Saturday moment." In the Catholic liturgy, Holy Saturday is the day after Good Friday and before Easter Sunday. Churches are left bare. No Mass is celebrated. Quiet pervades.

These in-between times are tough because nothing seems to be happening and we feel stuck. The very understandable temptation is to get unstuck by getting busy, distracting ourselves with various amusements, or latching on to a quick fix. If we resist the temptation, though, and become still for a while, welcoming such tender moments as gifts and not being afraid, we may grow in wisdom and understanding and find unexpected peace. It takes time for loneliness to become nourishing solitude, where such gifts await. In the *Four Quartets*, T. S. Eliot observes that after great loss, we often do not know what to ask or hope for. We thus have to let those desires and hopes incubate for a while, lest we ask for the wrong thing or what will ultimately not fulfill us. Sometimes, faith, hope, and love "are all in the waiting," Eliot wisely writes.

We cannot rush Easter. Freed from the need to figure out everything and do something *right now*, we give ourselves permission just to "be" for a while, so our thoughts and hopes can take shape.

For such moments, the Irish poet John O'Donohue offers a blessing: "May the absences in your life grow full of eternal echo." That echo stirs our imagination. "The lovely thing about the imagination," O'Donohue writes, "is that, whereas the mind often sees change and thinks everything is lost, the imagination can always go deeper than the actual experience of the loss and find something else in it."

All is not lost, although it may feel that way. Just as life percolates under the frozen ground and barren trees of winter, new life is stirring in times of loss. We are empty so we can be filled again; one dream has died so another can take shape. Such depth of living inspires hope, and hope, in the words of the poet Alexander Pope, "springs eternal in the human breast."

Enduring the pain of our Good Fridays or the emptiness of our Holy Saturdays is not easy. The temptation to run away, to anesthetize or insulate ourselves from the pain, is understandable but not helpful in the end. Although we should avoid unnecessary suffering, we do well to tend to, even befriend, our suffering. One of our default settings—which is both mysterious and frustrating—is that suffering can teach us important lessons. The Franciscan theologian and spiritual guide Richard Rohr offers this very helpful and honest counsel:

> *If we do not transform our pain, we will most assuredly transmit it*—usually to those closest to us: our family, our neighbors, our co-workers, and, invariably, the most vulnerable, our children. . . . We shouldn't try to get rid of our own pain until we've learned what it has to teach. When we can hold our pain consciously and trustfully (and not project it elsewhere), we find ourselves in a very special liminal space. Here we are open to learning and breaking through to a much deeper level of faith and consciousness. Please trust me on this. We must all *carry the cross of our own reality* until God transforms us through it. *These are the wounded healers of the world, and healers who have fully faced their wounds are the only ones who heal anyone else.*

The lessons we learn in the school of suffering hold wisdom as their promise. Such wisdom is hard-earned but ultimately a gift. On the night

Martin Luther King Jr. was assassinated, Robert Kennedy invoked the words of the Greek poet Aeschylus to comfort a heartsick and shocked nation: "In our sleep, pain which cannot forget falls drop by drop upon the heart until, in our own despair, against our will, comes wisdom through the awful grace of God."

In times of suffering and loss in my life, I have experienced such "awful grace" in different ways, even though I might have appreciated that wisdom only after the pain subsided. For example, I was reminded of the people in my life who really mattered and whom I sadly took for granted in better times. In my powerlessness in the face of events I could not ultimately control, I was freed (at least for a time) from the arrogance that led me to think I could control everything, and I learned to trust others more. I realized, too, how I tried to find security in things that really do not matter in the end—material possessions, titles, honors, positions of authority—and in their place, I heard God's word to me: you are loved for who you are, not what you do or have. When sitting with a broken heart, I learned that sometimes only when a heart is broken does it have room to expand.

Above all, as Rohr points out, suffering has made me more compassionate to others, whose pain I did not fully appreciate but now can better understand. All of us carry around crosses that we do not choose but are given to us. They are often invisible to others, which can make them even heavier. When we access our own pain, we begin to see the crosses of others. Upon seeing them, we can assume the role of a man named Simon who long ago helped Jesus carry his cross on the road to Calvary, before slipping back into anonymity (Matthew 27:32; Mark 15:21; Luke 23:26). Helping one another carry our crosses, we are strengthened in a school of solidarity. Even in pain, we taste a bit of the joy that comes with kinship.

Sometimes, even wisdom is elusive, and the best we can do is to just keep walking. On our Good Fridays, when suffering of mind, body, or spirit almost overwhelms, we just keep moving forward. On our Holy Saturdays, as we cross barren and lonely terrain, we just keep walking. Perseverance is an underappreciated grace because it is so difficult, but it is still grace, a help that comes from God and our inner strength. In his diaries, Dag Hammarskjöld, former secretary-general of the United Nations and Nobel Peace Prize winner, noted the ordinary heroism of such moments: "Only one feat is possible—not to have run away." An old adage attributed to Winston Churchill rings true: "If you're going through hell, keep going!" We dig deep down, and tap into whatever resilience, grit, or courage we can muster, and take the next step, even if it is in the darkness. In his poem "For Courage," John O'Donohue offers this encouragement:

> Know that you are not alone
> And that this darkness has purpose;
> Gradually it will school your eyes
> To find the one gift your life requires
> Hidden within this night-corner.

## Choosing Hope

If we just keep walking, learning, and living deeply, hope will come. Hope is the virtue of the pilgrim, impelling us to keep going in difficult times. In his last speech before he was assassinated, Martin Luther King Jr. said, "Only when it is dark enough can you see the stars."

Hope deepens our vision so that we can see a glimmer of light in the darkness. Hope liberates us to imagine a future different from our present. However bound we are by bodily pain or current circumstances, hope lifts our spirit to higher ground. The American poet Emily Dickinson describes this soaring hope:

> Hope is the thing with feathers
> That perches in the soul
> And sings the tune without words.
> And never stops—at all.

Hope is not the same as optimism, which too quickly glosses over reality and assumes everything will be fine. Vaclav Havel, a playwright and former president of the Czech Republic, described the difference: "Hope is not the conviction that something will turn out well, but the certainty that something makes sense, regardless of how it turns out." In *Man's Search for Meaning*, an extended reflection on his and others' experience in Hitler's concentration camps, Viktor Frankl wrote that while we cannot avoid suffering, we retain the spiritual freedom to choose how to respond to it: "The way in which a man accepts his fate and all the sufferings it entails, the way in which he takes up his cross, gives him ample opportunity—even under the most difficult circumstances—to add a deeper meaning to his life."

While sometimes hope is a gift unexpectedly given to us, we can also choose to hope. Warm feelings may not accompany those choices at first, but as Timothy Radcliffe points out, "by expressing a hope, it brings it nearer." Choosing hope, we live differently. Hope insists that things do not have to be this way and motivates us to do something about it if we can. Bryan Stevenson is the founder of the Equal Justice Initiative, an advocate for those in prison and on death row, and the author of *Just Mercy*, a best seller later made into a popular movie. Stevenson has witnessed firsthand the transformative power of hope. "We've been dealing with injustice in so many places, for so long," he said in a podcast interview. "And if you try to dissect, why is this still here?, it's because people haven't had enough hope and confidence to believe that we can do something better. You know, I think hope is our superpower. I mean, hope is the thing that gets you to stand up when others say, Sit down. It's the thing that gets you to speak when others say, Be quiet."

For more than thirty years, Stevenson and his team have contested wrongful convictions and unjust sentences and challenged the assumptions that have led to mass incarceration in this country. They have seen many successes, but even when they fail, they keep going, driven by hope. In 2018, Stevenson's organization opened the National Memorial for Peace and Justice in Montgomery, Alabama, which sits on a hill on a six-acre site not far from the state capitol. The memorial testifies to the 4,300 lynchings of Black persons in the United States between 1877 and 1950. A reverent silence pervades the mostly open-air memorial. Over eight hundred six-foot-tall steel monuments hang from the ceilings, one for each county where lynchings have been recorded.

When visiting the memorial with a group of graduate students shortly after it opened, I searched for the monument for my home county in Florida. The names of Samuel Nelson and Henry Simmons, both killed in the 1920s in Palm Beach County, are etched there. Before leaving, I paused to soak in the words on a plaque with the museum's dedication, which so powerfully ties together hope and other virtues:

> For the hanged and beaten.
> For the shot, drowned, and burned.
> For the tortured, tormented, and terrorized.
> For those abandoned by the rule of law.
> We will remember.
> With hope because hopelessness is the enemy of justice.
> With courage because peace requires bravery.
> With persistence because justice is a constant struggle.
> With faith because we shall overcome.

## Living the Easter Mystery

For Christians, Easter is the paramount source of hope, the preeminent example of love persevering. The Resurrection is the mystery of faith that proclaims that God raised Jesus from the dead. Easter is not just a good day for Jesus but for all of creation because in the Resurrection, life ultimately prevails over death, love over hate, peace over violence. What got Jesus killed—the reign of justice, peace, and love—is vindicated. According to the Anglican bishop and scholar N. T. Wright, "Resurrection is not the redescription of death; it is its overthrow and, with that, the overthrow of those whose power depends on it."

Around the time of Jesus, some Jews believed in resurrection as a communal event at the end of time, when God would reward the just and right all wrongs. The Gospel narratives develop this doctrine significantly. In Jesus raised from the dead, resurrection is personal (it happens to Jesus) and takes place now (not at the end of time). Resurrection is more than just "going to heaven"; it is about God's work of ushering in what the Scriptures describe as a new heaven and a new earth (Isaiah 65:17; 2 Peter 3:13; Revelation 21:1). This does not mean that God hits the delete button and starts over. Far from it. All creation is freed from its limits, realizing its awesome potential and making all things new (Revelation 21:5). In N. T. Wright's words, "Easter is about the wild delight of God's creative power." God is up to something new and wonderful: "Jesus' resurrection is the beginning of God's new project not to snatch people away from earth to heaven but to colonize earth with the life of heaven." Hope summons us to join in the holy and human labor of creating a new heaven and a new earth. It is the fuel for our labors for justice.

Understandably, the Gospel writers strain to capture in words this newness, this mystery, but they give us clues. For example, all four Gospels indicate that the disciples came to Jesus' tomb, which they discover empty, at the dawn of the first day of the week (Matthew 28:1; Mark 16:2; Luke 24:1; John 20:1). This description harks back to the book of Genesis, when on the first day of creation, God creates the heavens and the earth and pronounces, "Let there be light" (1:1–5). Easter is the dawn of another creation, as profound and glorious as the first creation.

Furthermore, the Gospels portray the risen Jesus in ways both familiar and new. Some of his friends recognize him while others do not (for example, he is mistaken for a gardener in John's Gospel and a stranger on the road in Luke's Gospel). He eats, speaks, and walks, but he can also suddenly appear out of nowhere. Because he has a body and does bodily things, the risen Jesus is not a ghost, yet his physicality is different from ours. Resurrection is thus not Jesus' soul escaping his body. He does not simply jettison his humanity on the way to heaven, like Clark Kent ripping off his human business suit as he becomes Superman. His body is part of this new creation, which means that all that is physical—all of creation—is caught up in God's redeeming Easter activity. This affirmation of the physical has profound implications: our bodies and all matter have eternal significance, demanding reverence for the human person, human bodies, and the natural world.

Equally compelling for me is that the risen Jesus shows up with the wounds of the crucifixion still on him (Luke 24:39–40; John 20:24–29). As a very practical point, this detail shows that the one appearing is the same as the one crucified. Yet it means so much more. In God's wisdom and tenderness, Jesus' marks of suffering remain as a sign that Jesus' humanity is part of this new creation. Our humanity includes the wounds we carry, which shape, who we are. To lose them is to lose part of our identity. At the same time, in the risen life, those wounds are redeemed. Their pain no longer has a hold on us.

What is heaven, then, for the Christian? Because of its newness, we can use only images and metaphors. One unhelpful image, at least for me, is that heaven is what comes *after* this life, as if heaven were on the same time-line as this life. N. T. Wright offers a more appealing perspective: "Heaven, in the Bible, is not a future destiny but the other, hidden, dimension of our ordinary life—God's dimension, if you like, God made heaven and earth; at the last he will remake both and join them together forever."

Heaven is around us more than beyond us, somewhere in the distance. The challenge is for us to see deeply enough to notice it. Emily Dickinson wrote:

> Who has not found the heaven—below—
> Will fail of it above.—
> God's residence is next to mine,
> His furniture is love.

In the Celtic Irish imagination, we live amid "thin places" where the veil between heaven and Earth is porous. This closeness is portrayed beautifully in churches with depictions of saints in stained-glass windows. In such sacred spaces, even when alone, I feel surrounded by my family in faith, enfolding me in their love and encouragement.

Drawing from his Jewish roots, Jesus proposed an image of heaven that resonates deeply with me: heaven is like a banquet or a wedding feast (Matthew 22:1–14; Luke 14:15–24). Recall his parable of the prodigal son, which ends in a feast. The Gospels portray Jesus eating a lot and dining with all sorts of people. He eats in the risen life too, even cooking breakfast for his disciples (John 21:1–14). Now that's a God I can relate to! For me, heaven is loud, full of conversation and laughter, and lively music (no harps, please!). And there are people I know and people I do not, but we are all friends, sharing a sumptuous meal at a table that grows spacious enough for everyone. Long before Jesus' time, the Jewish prophet Isaiah imagines such a feast, taking place on God's holy mountain in Jerusalem, a symbol of closeness to God:

> On this mountain the lord of hosts
> will provide for all peoples
> A feast of rich food and choice wines,
> juicy, rich food and pure, choice wines.
> On this mountain he will destroy
> the veil that veils all peoples,
> The web that is woven over all nations.
> He will destroy death forever.
> The Lord God will wipe away
> the tears from all faces.
>
> —Isaiah 25:6–8

My parents and other loved ones are part of the communion of saints at that banquet. They love me still, in the love of God that binds heaven and Earth. Sometimes, I can hear echoes of their laughter at the heavenly banquet during meals on this side of heaven, at the eucharistic meal at Mass, or a dinner at home with friends.

# Becoming Consolers in Action

St. Ignatius devotes the last portion of the Spiritual Exercises to praying with Jesus in his resurrected life, that is, through various accounts of the resurrection in the Gospels. Ignatius asks us to focus on a particular aspect of the risen Jesus: look at how he consoles people, as friends console one another (SE 224). We keep learning from Jesus. If we want to realize the hidden, heavenly dimension of our earthly life, then we ought to do what Jesus did: console people, encourage people. This is practicing hope, which brings it nearer.

Ignatius includes a tender meditation to open this part of the Exercises. He constructs an exercise that is not found in the Bible but makes perfect sense: before anyone else, the risen Jesus visits his mother to console her (SE 219, 299). In other contemplations, Ignatius relies on accounts found in Scripture. He invites us to pray for the grace to experience the joy that the risen Jesus offers those he meets (SE 221). This joy is much deeper than happiness, which can be induced (try chocolate ice cream!) and fleeting. Joy is the hidden gemstone sometimes found under the residue of our suffering, when hope seeps through the cracks and crevices of our lives.

I find particularly moving the story of the two disciples on the road to Emmaus, a village not far from Jerusalem, after the Crucifixion (Luke 24:13–35). They are walking away from Jerusalem, confused and dejected. The risen Jesus approaches them, but they do not recognize him. He walks with them and listens as they struggle to make sense of the Passion, the cross, the empty tomb. After listening for a while, Jesus starts to explain the meaning of it all, offering them hope. When they reach the village, the two friends ask the stranger to stay with them to share a meal. As Jesus breaks bread with them, they recognize him, but then he vanishes. "Were not our hearts burning within us while he spoke to us on the way and opened the scriptures to us?" they exclaim. With joy now, they return to Jerusalem to share with the other disciples all they had experienced on the road. Having been consoled, they console others. Their burning hearts, filled over the brim with love, are a reminder that heaven is near.

Those disciples go back to the familiar territory of Jerusalem, but they are different. "Grief does not leave you where it found you," my friend Greg once told me as I was struggling with a significant loss in my life. His words gave me hope that things would get better. With time they did, but I was also changed. In her book *The Other Side of Chaos*, Margaret Silf reminds us that in the story of Noah, after the great flood, they did not return to the same place as before. The ark landed in a new place, on the top of a mountain (Genesis 8:1–4): "The ark comes to rest at a higher place than it could possibly have reached had it not been carried there on the waters of apparent destruction."

The poet was right: hope is the thing with feathers that takes us to a higher place. We would never seek this plane because the journey there is much too hard. Yet, remarkably, we find ourselves grateful for having landed there because we are transformed. In her remarkable life, the Swiss psychiatrist Elisabeth Kübler-Ross helped countless people navigate the difficult terrain of grief and find meaning in loss. She wrote:

> The most beautiful people we have known are those who have known defeat, known suffering, known struggle, known loss, and have found their way out of the depths. These persons have an appreciation, a sensitivity, and an understanding of life that fills them with compassion, gentleness, and a deep loving concern. Beautiful people do not just happen.

Beautiful people do not just happen; they are made. They are suffering's unexpected contribution—even blessing—to the new heaven and new earth that we await and work for with great hope.

# Spiritual Exercises

- If you are suffering, and wish to lament, prayerfully read or give voice to one or more of the following Psalms from the Old Testament: 6, 22, 31, 38, 42, 102. Or write your own psalm of lament in your journal. Be real. God can take it.

- Practice stillness by paying attention to your breathing. Breathe in and out, deep, slow breaths, from the depth of your body. Breathe in, extending your belly. Hold for a moment. Then breathe out, slowly, emptying your lungs. Just as we need to empty our lungs for them to be filled with fresh air, sometimes our lives become empty so that they may be filled in new ways. Imagine your life emptying and being filled again.

- Reflect on a time of suffering or loss you have endured. What did you learn from the experience? Who was important to you during this time?

- Use your imagination and pray with the resurrection narratives from the Gospel. For example, accompany Mary Magdalene when she meets Jesus, her friend, in the garden (John 20:1–18); witness Thomas in his struggle with doubt and belief (John 20:19–29); join the apostles as they go fishing and meet the risen Jesus, and as they share breakfast by the shore (John 21:1–19); walk with two disciples as they meet Jesus on the road to Emmaus and share a meal (Luke 24:13–35). Notice how Jesus meets people where they are to offer them what they uniquely need. What good news does Jesus want to give you? How does he want to console or encourage you?

- Consider someone you know who needs encouragement. How can you console or encourage them? How can you accompany them?

# Chapter 8

# LIVING WITH DISCERNMENT

## Growing in Spiritual Wisdom and Making Good Decisions

I would not be here were it not for a Jesuit.

My mom and dad were born and raised in Montreal and came from very different worlds. My father, Larry O'Brien, never went to college. Instead, he started to work for the local English-language newspaper and eventually became a sportswriter and hosted a popular radio show in Montreal. As his last name indicates, Larry was working-class Irish. My mother, Elizabeth Fleming—or "Libby," as she was known—was from a well-established family in Montreal and known in more elite social circles. The Flemings were also Scotch Presbyterians, and very active ones. They had a pew in one of the most beautiful churches on Sherbrooke Street in downtown Montreal. Both my mom and dad had outgoing personalities and loved a crowd. Their circle of friends was wide. By my mother's telling at least, she had to give my dad an ultimatum as their lively courtship grew more extended. A few years younger but in her thirties, she wanted to marry but did not want to wait much longer. Approaching forty, Larry wisely saw the light, and they became engaged.

One problem though: she was Protestant and he was Catholic. And this was 1960, when the ecumenical movement, though growing, was not yet mainstream, as it would later become with the impetus of the Second Vatican Council (1962–1965) and other theological movements. In a conversation a few years before she died, my mother told me that the pastor of her church would not marry her because she was marrying a Catholic, a position also common among Catholic priests at that time.

Enter the Jesuit. My uncle had attended the Jesuit high school in the neighborhood where he and my dad grew up on the west side of Montreal. So my father asked a Jesuit at Loyola College, Lionel Stanford, SJ, if he would preside at the wedding. Fr. Stanford agreed, and the wedding took place on a cold January day in 1961 in the college chapel.

The first time I heard about Fr. Stanford was soon after I told my parents that I was going to join the Jesuits. I was then twenty-eight years old and teaching at a local Catholic high school after a brief stint practicing law. Given the various detours that marked my twenties, my parents received the news with some caution at first. My mom, though, was more reticent. I had gone to Georgetown, so she knew my Jesuit friends from there and enjoyed their company. She liked how down-to-earth and gregarious they were, and they always made her feel comfortable in Catholic circles. So I wondered what her hesitation was about. Turns out that Fr. Stanford's brother, Maurice, also a Jesuit, was sent to northeastern India as a young missionary priest and spent the rest of his life there—not exactly what my mother had in mind for me.

After I explained how Jesuit ministry had evolved over the decades, she felt better, and because I wanted to be an educator, like Jesuits I admired, I would likely serve in North America. Ironically, during one of my first summers as a younger Jesuit, I was asked to go to northeastern India to work in a leprosy hospital for a few months. "It's just a summer, Mom. Just a summer," I had to assure her a few times. To my delight, when in India, I met some Canadian Jesuits who knew Maurice Stanford, much beloved for his work at the Jesuit college in Darjeeling.

The only image I have of the priest who married my parents comes from a fading, black-and-white wedding photo. My parents stand on one side of the picture. My mom is beaming, beautiful in her white dress. My dad is smiling too in his black suit. They are both looking over at Fr. Stanford, standing next to them, his face with an expression of delight, laughing.

When my father approached him, Fr. Stanford could have said no. At the time, traditional theology and pastoral practice had plenty of arguments—bad ones, it turns out—that restricted the sacrament of matrimony only to Catholics. Beginning in the early twentieth century, a small but persuasive band of Catholic and Protestant theologians began to develop a more expansive view of the church. The Church of Christ was not limited to one particular denomination—for example, Catholic or Protestant—it embraced all those who were baptized and lived the Gospel. And marriage was not simply a means for Catholics to create (or procreate, in Catholic lingo) more Catholics, but also a way for the couple to deepen their love for one another as a concrete, tangible sign of God's unconditional love for us. That kind of love, given to all of God's children, could be shared between people of different faith traditions.

Although I never met him, I have often thought about Fr. Stanford as I now prepare couples—mostly my former students—for marriage. The Catholic tradition today has a fairly expansive view of marriage, permitting Catholics to marry those from other religions or no particular religion. To make the non-Catholic party feel more comfortable, I always tell the story of how I was raised by a Catholic father and Presbyterian mother, married by a Jesuit who was discerning enough to let go of old conventions and biases and say yes to helping a not-so-young couple from different faith backgrounds.

In this chapter, we reflect on discernment. Although Ignatius did not invent discernment—it is steeped in the biblical and Christian tradition—he contemporized it and made it accessible to people across the ages. Some of us may rely on elements of discernment without realizing it, such as when we rely on our intuition or "gut," notice negative instincts at play, or pray before or after making a decision. With Ignatian discernment, we are more intentional in our decision-making so that our decisions reflect the truth of who we are and who God calls us to be. Ignatian discernment is appealing because it is very practical, in keeping with the overall tenor of the Spiritual Exercises. It takes reality seriously, with all its complexities. I imagine that Fr. Stanford relied on Ignatian discernment to figure out how he would respond to my parents' request in the uniqueness of their situation.

It is fitting that discernment is our last topic of inquiry because it has been weaving in and out of the pages of this book, just below the surface. Discernment in the Ignatian tradition is not our destination or end, but how we get there. Discernment helps us sort through our restlessness, live the questions (particularly the difficult ones), honor our great and holy desires, and find meaning in our suffering. It helps us live more deeply, reflecting rather than simply reacting. With a discerning mind and heart, we courageously name our unfreedoms and chart the path to greater freedom for service and care of others. Discernment helps us see and respond to another's need so that our compassion yields effective action and builds relationships of kinship. Ignatian discernment is a sturdy rudder that allows us to navigate the various currents on our pilgrim journey.

# Defining Discernment

We begin by framing our discussion about discernment with some theological assumptions, referenced earlier in the book. In the Spiritual Exercises, St. Ignatius presents God as dwelling and laboring in creation for our good. This is a movement of divine love. In the Christian tradition, the divine in-dwelling and loving activity of God in creation is the Holy Spirit. Out of love, God communicates with us through what God has created, both in the world around us and in our interior life. Discernment helps us notice and interpret God's self-communication so that we can respond in a way that is "in sync" with God's gracious outreach. By coming to know and love Jesus, Christians pray to have a discerning heart like Jesus, who was completely in sync with God's desire for us.

With this background in mind, we define discernment in two ways: discernment of spirits and discernment of a choice. In one sense, discernment is spiritual sensitivity that allows a person to distinguish between what comes from God and what does not. One of the tremendous benefits of making the Spiritual Exercises in some form is becoming familiar with

Ignatius's "Rules for the Discernment of Spirits," part of the text of the *Exercises*. Though written five hundred years ago, Ignatius's rules remain helpful guidelines for us today and are accessible to people who are not religiously affiliated. These guidelines distinguish different interior movements (or spirits) that we commonly experience, so that we can understand what is happening in our spiritual life and make decisions reflective of who we are and want to be.

The practical application of the rules for discernment points us to a second and more common meaning of discernment as a process by which we make decisions about our life. Discernment is decision-making in which God is part of the conversation. In his book *Let Us Dream*, an extended reflection on the meaning of the COVID-19 pandemic for the world, Pope Francis writes that when we discern, "we humbly set before God the challenge we face, and ask for help," knowing that God wants to help us and is with us as we try to figure things out. With greater awareness of spiritual movements, we can make decisions with more confidence that they align with what God wants for us and our world.

Before diving more deeply into the practice of discernment, let me offer a few more preliminary points.

**First, the two meanings of discernment are related.** Discernment of a choice relies on our ability to discern the spirits, those interior movements we experience. The better we distinguish between what is and what is not of God, the better decisions we will make.

**Second, not every decision requires discernment.** I love food and thus have a hard time ordering at a restaurant because I want to try everything! A very good and patient friend of mine, having endured my ordering ritual too many times, once chided me: "Kevin, you don't need to discern between the pasta and the fish. Just decide!" God gifts us with intuition and practical knowledge, which we can also rely on.

**Third, discernment is reserved only for choosing among good alternatives.** There is no need to discern between robbing a bank and going to a movie: the moral choice is clear. Of course, given the complexity of life, we may not understand whether something is right or wrong, in which case discernment is a handy tool to have around. For example, despite my friend's urgent plea, I may need to discern between ordering steak or pasta if I am considering becoming a vegetarian as part of my moral commitment to care for the environment.

**Fourth, what we discern may be related to large or small matters.** Ignatius has a particular term for discerning a significant life choice or direction: an "election." For such important decisions, he outlines specific approaches, which we will review later. My parents' decision to get married, for example, would be a fitting subject for an election. Fr. Stanford's discernment about whether to help my parents and how to help them would be the more ordinary kind of discernment.

**Fifth, Ignatian discernment is a tool for both individuals and groups.** Because God labors in all things, we can discern the Spirit, the loving activity of God, in and around us. We can listen to our own hearts as well as listen to another's experience of God laboring in and through them. Discernment in common is not simply the sum of individual discernments of people in a group, but an awareness of how the spirits are moving within the group as a whole.

**Finally, while discernment is necessarily introspective, it is not intended to be a self-involved exercise.** Pope Francis, who knows discernment well from his decades of practicing and teaching discernment as a Jesuit, emphasizes this point: "Discernment, then, is not a solipsistic self-analysis or a form of egotistical introspection, but an authentic process of leaving ourselves behind in order to approach the mystery of God, who helps us to carry out the mission to which he has called us, for the good of our brothers and sisters" (GE 175).

# Recognizing Consolation and Desolation

We now turn to a more in-depth examination of what Ignatius means by the discernment of spirits. In Ignatian parlance, we refer to two kinds of spirits, reflecting their origin: the good spirit (or Holy Spirit, or angel of. light) is from God, and the evil spirit (or the bad spirit, or the enemy) is not.

The word *spirits* and Ignatius's reference to good and evil spirits may be distracting for some, conjuring images of horror films and demonic possession. Such language was not foreign to Ignatius's medieval imagination. In Jesus' own time, human beings were thought to live in a world where good and bad spirits were constantly at play, invoked to explain a host of human behaviors or physical phenomena. Today, we know much more about human motivations and the influence of culture and groups on how we make decisions. We also have many more scientific explanations for what happens in the world. Still, Ignatius's language of good and evil spirits is helpful because it recognizes that evil exists today in many forms. Evil is both part of who we are and greater than who we are. In the Exercises, Ignatius asks us to imagine good and evil as engaged in both a cosmic battle and a contest within the human heart. Discernment helps us understand these dynamics and navigate our conflicted hearts.

Regardless of how we label them, we experience these spirits as movements of the soul. These interior movements include thoughts, imaginings, emotions, inclinations, desires, feelings, repulsions, and attractions. Recall Ignatius's life-altering experience after his run-in with a cannonball at Pamplona. Stuck in bed during months of convalescence, Ignatius began to notice different interior movements as he imagined his future. In his autobiography, Ignatius writes (in the third person):

> He did not consider nor did he stop to examine this difference until one day his eyes were partially opened and he began to wonder at this difference and to reflect upon it. From experience he knew that some thoughts left him sad while others made him happy, and little by little he came to perceive the different spirits that were moving him; one coming from the devil, the other coming from God.

In Ignatian discernment, these disparate spiritual movements are characterized as either consolation or desolation. Consolation is an experience of being filled with love and gratitude. In consolation, we feel more alive, connected to God and others, and at peace with ourselves. We experience deep desires to help people. In Ignatius's words, "I call consolation every increase of faith, hope, and love, and all interior joy that invites and attracts to what is heavenly and to the salvation of one's soul by filling it with peace and quiet in its Creator and Lord" (SE 316). Desolation is the opposite. We feel disconnected from God and others and are mired in self-preoccupations. The soul is in heavy darkness or turmoil. We are bombarded by all sorts of doubts and temptations and are excessively restless and anxious as a result. Such movements, in Ignatius's words, dissipate our faith, hope, and love: "The soul is wholly slothful, tepid, sad, and separated, as it were, from its Creator and Lord" (SE 317).

Identifying a movement as consolation or desolation is vital because, according to Ignatius's rules, they call for different responses from us. Identifying them is not as easy as saying, "I'm happy, so I must be in consolation," or "I'm sad, so I must be in desolation." That may usually be the case, but not always. Recall our extended reflection on suffering and loss. These are painful moments, but they still can be consoling moments, in the Ignatian sense. (We can call such movements "difficult consolation," to borrow from Mark Thibodeaux, SJ, a popular writer and practitioner of the Exercises.) Accompanying my parents as they died was very sad, but I also experienced a profound sense of peace in the intimacy I found with them and my family at that time. My sadness was not desolation, just difficult consolation.

Conversely, I can feel happy, but this happiness may be illusory, a form of self-deceit. I once lived in a Jesuit community where I occasionally shared meals with a group of people. I enjoyed their company and left the meals feeling happy, but I gradually grew unsettled. Reflecting more on these interactions, I realized that, too often, our laughter was at the expense of others. I felt happy, but I was actually experiencing false consolation, which is a form of desolation. Instead of rashly labeling a movement as consolation or desolation, we are wise to pause and ask, *Where does the movement come from? And where does it lead me?*

To help us consider these questions, Ignatius offers some important guidance: the spirits operate differently depending on the direction our life is generally heading. When we are caught up in a pattern of sin or dysfunction, closed off from God or others, or living in a way that is harmful for ourselves or others, the good spirit shakes us up as if trying to get our attention so that we will change course and repair relationships. In Ignatius's words, the good spirit "will rouse the sting of conscience and fill them with remorse" (SE 314). The unsettled feelings I described about my uncharitable banter at meals is an example of the good spirit stirring up healthy remorse. The bad spirit, however, wants nothing more than for us to continue in our destructive ways, so it tries to make us complacent, offering excuses and enticing us with further distractions and unhealthy pleasures (SE 314). Rationalization is a typical ploy in such cases: "Oh, it's harmless fun to talk about another behind their back."

The spirits change tactics when we change direction. When we are generally "in good space," with our life heading in the right direction, the good spirit wants to encourage us to continue growing in greater faith, hope, and love. In such times, the spirit strengthens, consoles, removes obstacles, and gives peace to us. I recently spent a weekend with old friends, after not seeing them for a long time, and have felt lighter and happier since, a sign the good spirit wants me to nurture such meaningful relationships and find more balance between work and play.

Conversely, the bad spirit wants to derail our progress by stirring up needless anxiety, inflicting sadness, unsettling the soul, and seducing us with fallacious reasoning (SE 315). Several times during that weekend with friends, I felt guilty that I was not working on this book! Guilt is an old trap for me. When I was younger, I felt guilty about a lot of things, so caught up was I in following rules and always feeling like I was falling short. Guilt or remorse is okay when we actually do something wrong. But feeling guilty about everything means that we do not appreciate what we *should* feel guilty about. As a result, we never really grow up or repair relationships. Plus, we end up living anxiously or with an abiding sense of gloom. This is exactly what the bad spirit wants! My wise and patient spiritual director, Howard, once told me that if the bad spirit cannot get us to sin, or break relationships, it will do everything it can to take away our joy.

Ignatius uses vivid imagery to paint the difference between how the spirits operate. In the case of fundamentally good people who are trying to live a good life, "the action of the good angel is delicate, gentle, delightful. It may be compared to a drop of water penetrating a sponge. The action of the evil spirit upon such souls is violent, noisy, and disturbing. It may be compared to a drop of water falling on a stone" (SE 335). I think most of us (especially if you are reading a book like this!) are heading in the right direction, trying to do the best we can. If we want shorthand for how the Holy Spirit operates, look for movements of deep peace, hopeful encouragement, and loving connection. Similarly, be wary of acting in times of discouragement, disquiet, fear, anxiety, and disconnection.

## Dealing with Desolation

In the "Rules," Ignatius offers specific advice about what we should do when experiencing consolation and desolation. His presumption is that everyone has spiritual ups and downs, which hopefully is a relief to us. Most of Ignatius's rules concern what to do with desolation because this is when we need the most help. One of his most important pieces of advice: in times of desolation, do not dramatically change course or make a big decision because the bad spirit is in charge. Ignatius advises, "For just as in consolation the good spirit guides and counsels us, so in desolation the evil spirit guides and counsels" (SE 318). This rule may make sense, but it is hard to follow because in times of desolation, we are understandably restless to do something to get us out of it.

Although we should not change our resolutions while in desolation, we do not have to be entirely passive in the face of the enemy's seductions. Remain faithful to prayer or spiritual practice, even increasing them if helpful (SE 319). Talk to a trusted friend or spiritual guide. Be gentle with yourself. Do anything that will help you remember God's faithfulness and your goodness. Even though it may feel like you are on your own, God has not left you and is strengthening you (SE 320, 324). Be patient and persevere because consolation will return, as it does in the normal ups and downs of anyone's spiritual life (SE 321). In times of consolation, Ignatius advises that we "store up" such consolations (SE 323). In doing so, when feeling desolate, we are less likely to become discouraged as we remember times of consolation that will return.

In his guide to Ignatian discernment, *God's Voice Within*, the Jesuit Mark Thibodeaux offers a helpful image that reinforces these points. Being human, we naturally deal with various disturbances of the soul. We cannot help but sometimes feel hurt, jealous, angry, or tempted. The challenge is not to indulge these feelings nor get too distracted by them. With experience, we know that these movements come and go. So, imagine, as Mark did, that you are on a long bus ride, and in the seat next to you, people get on and off the bus at different stops. That's the way anger is, for example: it comes and goes. When anger comes, let it sit quietly next to you, being attentive to it, but certainly not letting it get in the driver's seat. You know that it will get off the bus eventually. The rules for discernment teach us how we can nurture a quietness or equilibrium of soul so that we can see those desolations and distractions for what they are: part of us but not defining us.

God, who loves us and wants us to grow in faith, hope, and love, gifts us with consolation. God does not inflict desolation on us but does permit it to happen. Why does God allow us to suffer desolation? This is a similar question to what we explored in the earlier chapter on the meaning of suffering. Ignatius suggests three main causes for the spiritual desolation we suffer. His hope is that the more we understand these reasons, the less likely we are to become further distracted or discouraged when feeling desolate.

The first explanation is that spiritual desolation is a wake-up call when we have been lax in our spiritual practices or have settled for shallowness in our prayer (SE 322). Or, I would add, that desolation may be a sign that we have let important, nourishing relationships in our life languish, or that we are not taking care of ourselves.

Second, Ignatius explains, God permits desolation so that we can learn more about ourselves and our God and deepen our relationship. For example, experiences of desolation measure how much our spiritual life rests on feeling good (SE 322). As the author and spiritual director David Fleming, SJ, asks when interpreting this rule, Do we love God or do we just love the gifts of God? By persevering in times of desolation, we come to understand that faith involves more than feeling good; faith, like love, also has to do with steadfast commitment, which matures us emotionally and spiritually.

Ignatius's third explanation is that desolation is a moment to exercise humility (SE 322). Consolation is a gift from God, which we cannot force or fake. When things are going well, we can take consolation for granted. In desolation, we are reminded of God's gifts to us and our constant need for God and others. In desolation, we also learn to ask for help, letting go of the idol of self-sufficiency (SE 322, 324).

## Understanding the Tactics of the Evil Spirit

Reflecting on his own spiritual struggles, Ignatius recognized certain patterns of the bad spirit, which he described so that we, too, might recognize the deceits and traps of the bad spirit and respond constructively. In the text of the Exercises, Ignatius uses some outdated language and images, so I contemporize them with the help of Fr. Fleming, who was instrumental in making the Exercises more accessible to people in the decades after the Second Vatican Council.

The bad spirit can sometimes behave like a spoiled child (SE 325). When an adult is firm with a petulant child, the child usually gives up. But if an adult starts to indulge a quarreling child or shows weakness in any way, the child becomes even bolder and more unyielding in their demands. Similarly, the bad spirit will weaken when we boldly face its temptations or proactively act against them, doing the exact opposite of what the bad spirit is tempting us to do. But if we become disheartened or afraid, the bad spirit will only grow in influence over us. The underlying assumption of this rule is that the evil spirit is basically weak. Although the enemy may tempt us, we can resist if we summon our will and lean on God and others. In the face of our strength, the enemy cowers.

Earlier in my Jesuit life, I experienced a pattern of recurrent worries about the future. They were distractions from the joy I was experiencing in my present work and life as a Jesuit. My spiritual director, Gordon, offered an image that helped me understand what was happening. Imagine, he suggested, that you are on a subway platform. The subway arrives at the station, and the doors open. Imagine that inside the subway car are all those distracting feelings and preoccupations begging to be indulged. Keep your feet firmly planted on the platform because you know that the doors will close and that train will move on, without you.

Ignatius cautions that we must act against the temptations as soon as they begin, otherwise they can easily wear us down, much like a spoiled child can. Twelve-step programs offer some helpful advice to all of us. Be careful when you are hungry, angry, lonely, tired, or stressed—known as "HALTS." At such times, we are particularly vulnerable to the wiles of the evil spirit.

Another image that Ignatius offers us is that of the false lover, or one who uses another person for their selfish ends (SE 326). Selfish people try to keep their machinations hidden so that they can continue unabated on their destructive course. The needless doubts, confusion, insecurities, and anxiety that the bad spirit sows fester in the darkness. God operates differently, always wanting to bring light into the darkness.

My friend Michael confided in me about an addictive behavior that he managed to keep secret for many months. He also minimized the behavior to himself, justifying it as a necessary and harmless reward for all his good work. Only when he admitted his addictive habit to himself and to trusted friends did his recovery begin, which included a painful realization about how disruptive the addiction actually was. When we are in desolation, we may not feel like talking to anyone, fearing another's reaction or doubting that others want to listen to us. Freeing ourselves of the burden of silence can thus be a courageous choice. When this happens, trust displaces fear. Bringing our unfreedom to light unmasks the bad spirit and lessens its hold over us.

Finally, Ignatius proposes that the bad spirit acts like a military commander, mercilessly pursuing an objective in battle (SE 327). A military commander shrewdly assesses the strengths and weaknesses of his opponent and then attacks at the most vulnerable point. They search out the opponent's blind spots or any point of unpreparedness. When the opponent becomes too self-satisfied and lets down his guard, the commander begins the assault.

In the previous two images, Ignatius advises us about how to act when we discern the presence of the bad spirit: resist temptations from a position of strength and bring secrets and gnawing desolation to the light. Here, he suggests that we fortify our weakness before the enemy's onslaught. To do this, we must be self-aware and honest with ourselves about our weak spots: *When am I most susceptible to desolation? Which people, places, situations, or train of thought bring about desolation?* In our vulnerability, we are likely to cry out to God or to other people for help. However, when we are complacent or too proud, we can become slack in our vigilance and easily forget our need for help, which is just what the evil spirit wants. Without humility, we may ignore our weaknesses and open the door to desolation.

A particular weak spot for me is self-doubt and a perfectionist tendency that developed to overcompensate for that self-doubt. Over the years, I have learned to become more sensitive to these tendencies and have allowed others to hold me accountable. I've also acted against them by doing the opposite: receiving compliments more graciously, embracing failure as a path to learning and an occasional price for trying something new, and putting limits on my workaholic tendencies.

Remember Ignatius's fundamental premise: the enemy is weak, and grace always prevails, if we let it. With the gift of self-awareness, we can fortify our all-too-human weaknesses. The temptations, doubts, and fears may come, but they will not be able to take hold if we leave them no room. As we advance on the spiritual journey, we get in the habit of noticing the spirits that operate on our souls. We get better at naming spiritual desolation and acting against it, and we learn to run with the movements of the good spirit in times of consolation.

# Distinguishing between Authentic and False Consolation

Sometimes the evil spirit's tactics are obvious: causing extreme doubt, confusion, anxiety, and temptation for those striving to live a good life. As we grow spiritually, the enemy must adjust its tactics and become more subtle and wily to lure us off course. The bad spirit even uses experiences of spiritual consolation for evil ends and suggests thoughts that seem good and holy but that lead us away from our noble purpose. Quietly and almost imperceptibly, the enemy can distract us with good feelings and undermine an experience of consolation to cause spiritual harm (SE 331, 332). What begins as an experience of consolation ends—to our surprise—with desolation.

How can we tell whether we are dealing with authentic consolation, which is from God, or false consolation, which is from the enemy and a form of desolation?

Ignatius first answers that there are times when we are absolutely convinced that the consolation is of God, and not false. He calls this experience consolation "without any previous cause" (SE 330). This occurs when we are simply bowled over by grace, whether we are doing something explicitly religious (like praying) or not (like going for a walk). We are undeniably part of a Love greater than ourselves. We experience this kind of consolation almost as a complete surprise, for nothing we have thought, done, or intended has caused it. In such moments, the proper response is not to overanalyze or doubt, but to give thanks and enjoy!

While acknowledging the reality of such experiences, Ignatius injects a note of caution. Be careful, he says, of making any decision right after such powerful, insightful moments. Sometimes we can get carried away by the emotional high of the experience. Think of the exhilarating heights of romance: we do well to come down to earth before making any decision about marriage! If a resolution emerges during a time of consolation without a prior cause, carefully discern before acting on it (SE 336).

Whether this is a common occurrence or not is a subject of debate among practitioners of Ignatian spirituality. My hunch is that it happens more than we think, but we are too distracted by noise, clutter, and activity to notice. I remember doing something completely ordinary and nondescript with a friend, and suddenly becoming overwhelmed with gratitude for our friendship. I also remember a time as a young priest, walking back from the gym to say Mass at the parish where I was assigned. And in the middle of a crowded street, I just felt so strongly I was doing what God asked me to do. A sign of such experiences of consolation is that we lack words to adequately describe them.

It is more often the case that some thought, memory, experience, or encounter triggers consolation. The feeling does not come "out of the blue" but is connected to something we are doing or thinking. When that happens, we must discern carefully what has caused the consolation to determine whether it is authentic or false consolation. Ignatius writes: "It is a mark of the evil spirit to assume the appearance of an angel of light. He begins by suggesting thoughts that are suited to a devout soul, and ends by suggesting his own" (SE 332). For example, healthy confidence can devolve into arrogance and preoccupation with control; sincere piety and religious conviction can turn into self-righteousness and close-mindedness; enthusiasm can become diffuse and scattered rather than focused and effective.

After I was ordained, I was assigned to a large parish and school in Washington, DC. I loved the variety of ministry with people of all ages. As a relatively young and new priest, I was in demand. It felt good to be called upon to do lots of things. Affirmation came early and quickly. I was passionate about what I was doing, and people appreciated it. Energized by the people's faith, my own faith came alive in new ways. All this is good and consoling. But gradually the bad spirit corrupted that consolation. I loved the affirmation so much that I rarely said no to requests, which led to exhaustion. I sometimes hedged in giving difficult counsel to a person to avoid losing that person's affirmation and approval. I distinctly recall deleting a line from a homily because I thought it might alienate some people. In my zeal, I sometimes acted hastily, bypassing needed consultation that would have better served the parish.

Fortunately, I had a mentor who helped me identify the emergence of false consolation and change course. Note how clever the bad spirit is, coming to us under false pretenses as an "angel of light" (SE 332) but then disquieting us. Ignatius advises: "By destroying the peace, tranquility, and quiet which it had before, it may cause disturbance to the soul. These things are a clear sign that the thoughts are proceeding from the evil spirit, the enemy of our progress and eternal salvation" (SE 333). If we notice that a course of thinking or acting led us to a dead end despite our best intentions, we can make necessary changes, ask for forgiveness, and learn from our mistakes. "The purpose of this review," Ignatius explains, "is that once such an experience has been understood and carefully observed, we may guard ourselves for the future against the customary deceits of the enemy" (SE 334). This is difficult but graced awareness. How much better if we can notice how the enemy is roaming about *before* the damage is done!

The bottom line is that we can judge the spirit by its fruits: *Where did it lead us?* With time and effort, and the grace of God, we can better discern the spirits and in doing so savor authentic consolations, uncover false consolations, and resist acting out of desolation.

# Making Big Decisions

Thus far, we have been exploring discernment that takes place in our ordinary life. In the Exercises, Ignatius describes a related mode of discernment for making bigger decisions, traditionally called the *election* (SE 169–89). Making an election relies on the person having developed a practice of discernment in ordinary matters, as discussed above. Ignatius mentions as proper subjects for an election the choice of getting married or entering religious life. Over time, the Exercises have helped people make a wide array of other choices about career, family, relationships, and lifestyle. The election does not apply to basic decisions between right and wrong but to worthy commitments and choices between two or more good options (SE 170).

Earlier in the book, we discussed how central our image of God is in helping or hindering our spiritual journey. The God that Ignatius got to know over the course of his life was a helping and encouraging God. Recall one image he shared in his autobiography: God worked with him as a teacher working with a pupil. The Exercises are built on the foundation that God communicates with us uniquely and personally. God wants to help us make good choices so that we can thrive and become the person God created us to be. God is rooting for us, not testing us or abandoning us if we make a wrong decision. God remains with us even when we take a detour, helping us get back on course.

In making an election, Ignatius urges us to stay focused on our ultimate end (SE 169). As we discussed earlier, in the First Principle and Foundation exercise, Ignatius articulates one such end: we are created to know, love, and serve God and others (SE 23). We can devise our own mission statement, such as "to make the world a better place," "to care for my family," or "to serve the poor and forgotten." These are all noble ends with different avenues to achieving them. As we have learned, we need to be free with respect to those various avenues, choosing that which best helps us achieve our end.

We get into trouble, Ignatius observes, when we turn a means into an end and an end into a means. This happens when we become so fixated on a particular means that we short-circuit our discernment. Here's an example. At midlife, Luís, a successful businessman, was restless in his career. After raising his children, he had a deep desire to work more directly with economically disadvantaged communities, a laudable end. He also harbored a long-standing ambition to be a teacher, something he had never done. After some networking, he was offered a teaching position at a financially strapped high school, his dream job. At the same time, he was approached by the board chair of a local not-for-profit that incubated small businesses and mentored entrepreneurs to reinvest in their impoverished community.

They needed a new executive director, and Luis's qualifications matched their needs perfectly. Luís refused to consider the offer. He always wanted to be a teacher, so that's what he should do, he thought.

Luís was not free. He did not take the time to discern important questions: Which organization had the greater need for his talents? Which position would have a greater impact on serving people? Was he even good at teaching? Luís turned a means (teaching) into an end, and an end (working directly with poor communities) into a means, bending God's will to his own! In Ignatius's words, "Such persons do not go directly to God, but want God to conform wholly to their inordinate attachments" (SE 169).

With this initial caution in mind, Ignatius describes three situations in which a significant decision—that is, an election—is made. The first situation is a time of great clarity (SE 175). In circumstances dramatic or very ordinary, God shows us the course to follow with such decisiveness that we know with confidence that we are following God's lead. During this time, we are unable to doubt the rightness of the choice (although doubt may come later). This graced conviction is similar to an experience of consolation without a prior cause. We have to be careful that our clarity is sincere, and not, like in Luís's case, the result of refusing to consider other viable options.

The second situation lacks such indisputable clarity (SE 176). We experience opposing movements of certainty and doubt, of consolation and desolation. Such fluctuations are natural when making important decisions. Moreover, times of election are often moments of personal conversion, which we can simultaneously long for and resist. Here we apply the rules for the discernment of spirits, as described earlier. We want to choose and commit out of experiences of authentic spiritual consolation and avoid acting out of spiritual desolation.

In the third situation, we experience no strong movements one way or the other (SE 177–179). We are tranquil. To make a choice in this situation, we first ask God to help us. We try to be patient until the movements become clearer. We recall our fundamental purpose or end and strive to be open to the various options before us. We avoid temptations to short-circuit our discernment. For example, just because we feel something does not mean it is a desire we should follow. Desires need to be discerned. Or, just because one course is harder does not mean it is the better and more noble course (this is spiritual athleticism at its worse). The better way—the *magis*—is that which better serves one's fundamental end, whether easier or hard.

In this third mode of relative tranquility, Ignatius suggests some exercises to help us make a decision with greater confidence and clarity (SE 181–187). They are a mix of familiar mental reasoning and some novel imaginative exercises. Weigh the advantages and disadvantages of accepting a proposed course of action and the pros and cons of rejecting it. Or imagine what advice you would give someone else considering the same choice. Alternatively, imagine that you are on your deathbed or standing before God after your life has ended and talking with God about the decision you made. From those viewpoints, consider which choice you would want to have made now. These imaginative exercises free us from the confines of the present and offer a longer and different perspective that might clarify the values at stake in our decision and what, in the end, is most important to us.

Ignatius advises that, after making a decision, we pray for confirmation of the decision (SE 183). There is no set time for doing so. Although it is wise to pause as we seek confirmation, we should not delay decisions so much that we miss opportunities for growth and for doing good. In a culture that often runs from commitment, we pray for wisdom, prudence, and courage to make choices, especially hard ones, and then act on them.

Confirmation usually comes in the form of spiritual consolation, such as peace of mind, confidence, enthusiasm, creativity, hope, and closeness to God and others. If we experience undue anxiety, confusion, or sadness, we should refrain from acting in order to carefully discern those movements: Do they indicate that our election was somehow flawed? Or are they attempts by the bad spirit to distract us from doing what we are called to do?

Seeking confirmation has been pivotal in my own significant discernments. Very practically, it gives me time to consult trusted friends and mentors who know me. They often can see things that I miss because I am too close to the decision. With them, I step back and ask: *Does the decision make sense in the big picture? Does it fit into who I am and my overall life's direction?* I repeat, as if a mantra, a line from one of Gerard Manley Hopkins's poems: "What I do is me: for that I came." In other words, I want to choose and act from the deepest part of who I am. This is what it means to live with authenticity or integrity.

In addition to this Ignatian counsel when making significant decisions, I also rely on the advice of contemporary spiritual guides who offer shorthand versions of what Ignatius is getting at. Frederick Buechner, a popular theologian, writer, and Presbyterian minister, offers one of the most quoted definitions of vocation or one's calling in life: "The place God calls you to is the place where your deep gladness and the world's deep hunger meet." Similarly, the theologian and teacher Michael Himes distills discernment about a life's calling or vocation to the following three questions: What gives me joy? Am I good at it? Does the world need it? With their focus on joy and gladness, Himes and Buechner remind me that my deep desires are one way that God communicates God's desire for me.

Buechner and Himes also help me stay real and grounded. *Do I have the skills and talent to do what I am passionate about?* I love music and singing but will never become the lead singer in a band! I am just not that good (despite my stellar performances in the car). *Does the world need what I want to give?* Focusing on need is a very helpful criterion as we try to choose among equally good alternatives. Sifting the many needs presented to us, we can ask what the greater need is. This is what Ignatius does in the Constitutions of the Jesuits, the founding document of the Jesuit order. There he presents a list of criteria for deciding which ministries Jesuits would commit to. Among the chief criteria is the greater need: *Which needs are most urgent or grave? Is there anyone else qualified to address them?* The need question prevents discernment from devolving into self-preoccupation or navel-gazing and focuses us on serving others, which is what a vocation or calling is ultimately about.

# Growing in Spiritual Wisdom

As we conclude, let me summarize our deep dive into discernment. Discernment begins by our paying attention. We discern reality, not hypotheticals or abstractions. We pay attention to our experience (what is happening *around* us). This includes how God speaks to us through the beauty and brokenness of our world, or what the Second Vatican Council called the "signs of the times." We also pay attention to our interior reactions to that experience (what is happening *in* us). We identify interior movements of consolation and desolation and reflect on where they come from and where they lead us. With the help of Ignatius's rules for discernment, we understand how the good spirit and bad spirit operate so that we can follow the lead of the good spirit and reject the action of the bad spirit. We are honest with ourselves, knowing that the spirits will operate differently depending on where our life is heading. On the basis of this reflection, we make decisions. We then seek confirmation, and if we experience it, we take action, which may require its own discernment as we figure out *how* to achieve what we have decided to do. Finally, we step back and evaluate a discernment process so that we can learn from what we did right and where we got off track. Such evaluation helps us become more discerning and spiritually wise in the future.

Attention, reflection, decision, action, evaluation—these are the essential steps in Ignatian discernment. Discernment takes practice. The more we apply the rules to our lives, the more discerning a person we will become. Praying the Examen (as outlined in the Appendix) is a great way to practice discernment on a daily basis.

Ignatius's rules for the discernment of spirits and for an election are very practical, yet we cannot apply them formulaically and assume the "right" result simply because we followed the rules. The one doing the discerning is not a computer program but a person, with the usual mix of strengths and limitations, clarity and blind spots. Sometimes we can get in the way of discerning well. To become more spiritually wise, we can develop certain dispositions or virtues that, while not guaranteeing a sound discernment, make it much more likely.

**First, the discerner must have emotional maturity to attend to their interior life.** Although our feelings and desires are a natural part of who we are and tell us something about where we are on our journey, we are not what we feel. We need to distinguish our identity from our emotions (or mood or desires) so that we can properly discern them.

**Second, the discerner must have developed a habit of solitude so that they can discern the spirits.** For many, this means cultivating a prayer life in which they encounter Holy Mystery. This does not mean that we need to run away to a mountaintop but that we cultivate an inner quiet in the midst of activity or chaos that allows us to be sensitive to the movements in and around us and stay focused on our end. I love the image of Jesus presented in Mark's Gospel (4:35–41): he is in a boat with his disciples, crossing the sea, when a storm brews. While the winds rage and the waves crash over the boat, the Gospel writer notes that "Jesus was in the stern, asleep on a cushion." His frightened disciples wake him, and Jesus quiets the storm. "Why are you terrified?" he asks them. "Do you not yet have faith?" As we come to know and love Jesus, we learn his way of discerning reality. Discerners can remain calm and focused in any storm.

**Third, the discerner must exhibit freedom or indifference with respect to different means to the end they seek.** Of course, being human, we do not have to be perfectly free, just growing in freedom, or at least aware of "unfreedoms" that distract us from our ultimate aim.

**Fourth, the discerner must be patient.** In *Let Us Dream*, Pope Francis cautions that we must "resist the urge to seek the apparent relief of an immediate decision, and instead be willing to hold different options before the Lord." We need to cultivate "a healthy capacity for silent reflection, places of refuge from the tyranny of the urgent." Recall our reflection on Holy Saturday moments, those in-between times needed for our thinking, desiring, hoping, and imagining to ferment. If we avoid rushing a decision, then unexpected possibilities, novel solutions, and new dreams can emerge.

**Fifth, a good discerner must be courageous in dealing with the gray areas of life, which is most of life!** Discernment, Pope Francis writes, is difficult for those "who are allergic to uncertainty and want to reduce everything to black and white. And it is quite impossible for ideologues, fundamentalists, and anyone else who is held back by a rigid mindset." A discerner who is rigid in this way is not free; they are not open to new possibilities or breakthroughs in thinking. They are constrained by their fixation on the past and on their own plans for the future. Such persons are often legalistic in approaching conflict or messy situations and can be dismissive of people who think or act differently than they. Keeping distance, like those religious officials walking by the injured man in Jesus' parable of the good Samaritan, provides antiseptic clarity and comfort, but it comes at great cost. In choosing the other side of the road, they remove themselves from others and reject the invitation to love and be loved. Without such love, fear has plenty of room to grow.

When I was younger, I resisted the gray areas of life. Searching for the safety and security of the certain, I fought against ambiguity and was too often legalistic, defensive, and judgmental, like those Pharisees whom Jesus was continually trying to soften. But with time, I could not avoid the complexity of human living, including my own. Reality is complicated because we human beings are complicated, or in theological terms, we are mysteries created in the image of the God we call Holy Mystery. Pope Francis assures us, "Each person's situation before God and their life in grace are mysteries which no one can fully know from without" (EG 172). Get close to people and walk with them, the pope urges us. Enter in the maelstrom of human living, with all its pain and beauty. This is what Fr. Stanford did for my parents. In the gray, we, too, can rely on discernment to find our way and respond to human need. Perhaps the sign that we are discerning well is not clarity—at least at first—but compassion for the burdens that people carry. Sometimes the most generous response we can give when struggling to meet an ideal is an incomplete one, good enough for now.

**This brings us to a final disposition for a good discerner: humility.** We cannot control every complex situation, but we can control our response to it. We seek a discerning response, not a reactive, vindictive, or fainthearted one. Becoming spiritually wise, like any virtue, takes practice. We learn to discern the spirits by trial and error, which means that sometimes we will get it wrong, despite our best efforts. Even presuming a good discernment, there are no guarantees that we will be successful or be able to do what we want because other people are discerning and making decisions that impact us, and those decisions may conflict with ours (creating more of life's gray!). We may be certain, for example, that God is calling us to a particular job, but the hiring manager offers it to someone else. Ignatius was convinced that he was to spend his life in the Holy Land, but on his first try, he was ordered to leave, and later, with his companions, he was not able to find safe passage there. Such events should not undermine our confidence in the initial discernment, unless of course we later realize the discernment was undermined by the bad spirit. We do our best to follow God's lead, and then we trust that God is with us, wherever we land. God, who is generous and creative, will get us where we need to go, even if by a circuitous route.

In an interview early in his papacy, Pope Francis explained that discernment is so vital because our life is not given to us like a book in which everything is written down. Rather, life is more like an adventure in which we are searching for God and God is searching for us: "God is always a surprise, so you never know where and how you will find him." Adventure is an appealing metaphor for the process of discernment. Every worthwhile adventure has some unknown, some unpredictability, some mystery about it; that's why adventures are challenging yet also exciting! Life unfolds, the destination revealed more than dictated.

The art of discernment can also be compared to playing jazz, which is an adventurous form of music. In jazz, the musicians play a standard melody, and then they improvise. The piano player may start playing, but then the others join in: for example, the drummer, bass player, saxophonist. While the song begins with the familiar melody, it evolves as the other musicians change the chords and keys. For this to work, the musicians need to really pay attention to one another. What is remarkable about jazz is that no two performances are the same, unlike classical music, where musicians play the notes on the page with little noticeable difference from one performance to another. Jazz performances vary because improvisation is at the heart of jazz, the musicians playing off one another. An accomplished jazz musician has done his or her own hard work, which makes it possible to improvise with skill. At the same time, the musician has learned how to allow the music to evolve within the community of players.

I think that is how God works with us. Discernment is how we improvise with God and others. We do not follow unalterable sheet music or a script but play jazz with God. God provides a standard melody, and then we join in, with our talents, dreams, and desires. We improvise with what God has given us. For Christians, that means "riffing" on Jesus: embodying his values and way of living and loving, in the unique context of our particular lives. We listen to the music of the Spirit in our life, and we listen to what others are playing, and then we play: we choose, we act. God listens to our music, which is sometimes perfectly in tune, other times a little off key. Regardless, God works with us and plays some more, with new chords and keys, enlivening the familiar melody. And then we listen more and play again.

God's freedom and our freedom, as well as the freedom of others, are at play. Together, we can create something beautiful.

# Spiritual Exercises

- One practice in the Ignatian tradition of discernment is called the Examen. This spiritual exercise is a grateful review of the day, first thanking God for the gifts of the day, and then noticing the different movements of the spirit that we experienced. A daily practice of the Examen helps us become more grateful and more discerning. Try praying the Examen daily for one week, as a way of growing in discerning wisdom. See the Appendix for an outline of the Examen.

- Consider what consolation and desolation look or feel like in your life at the present. When or with whom do you normally experience consolation and desolation? What interior movements are usually associated with each?

- Are you approaching a significant decision in your life? Review Ignatius's steps for making an election and apply them to your particular decision. Or consider Himes's three questions: What gives me joy? Am I good at it? Does the world need it?

- Listen to jazz and feel the movement of the good spirit!

# Conclusion
## Love Persevering

Odysseus made it home to Ithaka where his beloved wife, Penelope, and son awaited him. His odyssey concludes with a happy ending (albeit not so happy for the many suitors of Penelope whom Odysseus killed in rage). That ending is more open ended than we tend to remember, for as the epic poem concludes, Odysseus recalls a prophecy that bids him to leave home again, on another journey. The British poet Alfred, Lord Tennyson elaborates on that summons in his beautiful poem "Ulysses," in which he imagines the restless hero ready to embark on his next adventure, rallying his compatriots to join him:

> Come, my friends,
> 'Tis not too late to seek a newer world. . . .
> Tho' much is taken, much abides; and tho'
> We are not now that strength which in old days
> Moved earth and heaven, that which we are, we are;
> One equal temper of heroic hearts,
> Made weak by time and fate, but strong in will
> To strive, to seek, to find, and not to yield.

As we walk with Ignatius through his Exercises, we hear a similar rallying cry that elicits a magnanimous response, and with it, hope. Like Odysseus's journeys, the Exercises are an adventure that never really ends because they conclude with an open-ended offering, a prayer that speaks to our heroic hearts:

> Take, Lord, and receive all my liberty, my memory, my under-
> standing, and my entire will—all that I have and call my own.
> You have given it all to me. To you, Lord, I return it. Everything
> is yours; do with it what you will. Give me only your love
> and your grace. That is enough for me. (SE 234, Fleming
> translation)

Having been loved so bountifully, we love in return. Grateful for all that God has given us, we just want to give back. Freed from the baggage that weighed us down, we are liberated to join the ongoing adventure of real-izing a new heaven and a new earth, which is already taking shape. God's dream for the world stirs in us great and noble desires to strive, seek, find, and never to yield.

The challenge, as we have recognized, is to look and live deeply enough to notice this newer world emerging. Giovanni Giocondo was a Franciscan friar and architect, involved in the construction of St. Peter's Basilica in Rome. In a Christmas letter to his friend in 1513, he wrote:

> Life is so generous a giver, but we, judging its gifts by their cov-
> erings, cast them away as ugly or heavy or hard. Remove the
> covering, and you will find beneath it a living splendor, woven
> of love, by wisdom, with power.
>
> Life is so full of meaning and of purpose, so full of
> beauty—beneath its covering—that you will find that earth but
> cloaks your heaven. Courage, then to claim it: that is all! But
> courage you have; and the knowledge that we are pilgrims
> together, wending through unknown country, home.

With depth of imagination, we begin to appreciate the many covered-over gifts in our lives.

We are pilgrims wending our way home in a world of grace, or river of grace. Courageously, we make our way down that river, with the Ignatian tradition of spirituality to guide us like a rudder among restless currents. Through this tradition, we cultivate habits of attentiveness, reflection, and discernment so that we can live with greater purpose and meaning. We learn to live gratefully and deeply, not Jet Skiing through life but scuba diving. We learn to see not just with our eyes but also with our heart, so that we can enjoy fields of dreams along the way. We give ourselves permission to take a long, loving look at the real, and stand, sit, or kneel in awe of the beauty and splendor around us, heaven bursting forth, holy ground (or water) shimmering everywhere.

God keeps trying to get our attention, awaiting a beholder, but too often we miss out. We are too busy staring down at our phones, or completing a checklist of "things to do," too busy building a résumé that we do not build a life. The newspaper columnist David Brooks writes that we spend way too much time fixating on "résumé virtues," those skills and achievements we amass to impress people, when instead we should be focused on cultivating "eulogy virtues," the attributes of character that people talk about at funerals and remember after we are gone. He's getting at the familiar adage: in the end, people will forget what you said, or what you did, but they will never forget how you made them feel. The Ignatian tradition helps us "course correct" so that we savor the journey. We then taste the freedom God wants to give us, so that we can make the final offering of the Exercises with every part of beautifully flawed selves, love pouring through the cracks, wounds redeemed as founts of compassion and holy boldness.

In a homily at a funeral Mass for a priest and four young men killed in his country's civil war, Óscar Romero said to the mourners, "In the evening of life you will be judged on love." He was paraphrasing the thought of the sixteenth-century Spanish mystic and poet St. John of the Cross, who gave us this very practical advice: "Where there is no love, put love and you will find love." We pilgrims are on the lookout not just for covered-over gifts to enjoy but for opportunities to plant love like seeds of the new heaven and new earth. What grows from them are the surest signs that we have passed through this life. Other marks of our journey—what we accomplished, the distance we traveled, or the attention we garnered—are just not as important or enduring as how we loved and were loved along the way and the community we formed with other pilgrims.

In the crucible of a concentration camp, Viktor Frankl learned the same lesson: the salvation of humanity is through and in love, he wrote. If you have made it this far in the book, you know that this love is not some mushy, saccharine kind of love. Love is a great feeling, but it is also a commitment that can cost us. As Father Zossima in Dostoevsky's *The Brothers Karamazov* observed, "Love in action is a harsh and dreadful thing compared with love in dreams." Love in action also takes time, as the fox and little prince discovered. They learned to tame each another, gradually, and then let one another go, their hearts forever changed and claimed. Love means loss too: that's the dreadful part of it. But if it's love, then there is gift too. Love perseveres.

Love is complicated because we are complicated. That which we are, we are: beautiful and broken, heroic and weak, sinners who are loved. We walk around shining like the sun, but shield our rubbled-over heart. At times, we can be as good as the Samaritan, so moved with compassion to help a stranger; at other times, we pass by on the other side of the road, afraid of getting too close. We accept the invitation to revel in the homecoming feast yet are also tempted to stew outside in resentment and self-righteousness. We live in Good Friday pain, Holy Saturday waiting, and Easter hope, all as interwoven as our lives. Pope Francis is right (again): our life is wonderfully complicated.

Dorothy Day, founder of the Catholic Worker movement, was profoundly in touch with beauty and brokenness, both in her own life and in the lives of people whom she met, served, and befriended at her houses of hospitality. At the conclusion of her autobiography, *The Long Loneliness*, she echoes Romero and Frankl's judgment about what matters most:

> The final word is love. At times it has been, in the words of
> Father Zossima, a harsh and dreadful thing, and our very faith

in love has been tried by fire. We cannot love God unless we love each other, and to love we must know each other. We know Him in the breaking of bread, and we know each other in the breaking of bread, and we are not alone any more. Heaven is a banquet and life is a banquet, too, even with a crust, where there is companionship. We have all known the long loneliness and we have learned that the only solution is love and that love comes with community.

Love is hard and complicated, but it is also our salvation. It pulls us out of our self-isolation and self-preoccupation and ties us to God, others, and all of creation. Love soothes our loneliness and salves the wounds we carry, whether they are hidden or apparent to all. We are not alone, enveloped as we are by the communion of saints, that is, people who tried their best, who feast in banquets and break bread together here and in heaven.

The final word *is* love, and love is both a verb and a noun. Ignatius's "First Principle and Foundation" provides the verb: we are created to love God and others, to love ourselves, and to love the natural world, in which the color purple blooms. Love is also a noun, another name for God who is Holy Mystery. God is the source of our loving—that holy desire deep down within our restless hearts—as well as its ultimate end and satisfaction. In between, we are blessed with the journey: one adventure, one question, folding into another, until we rest in grace, in that loving Mystery which summoned us all along.

# Appendix

## St. Ignatius's Prayer of Awareness: The Examen

The Examen is a tool that helps us develop habits central to the Spiritual Exercises, including gratitude, attentiveness, reflection, and discernment. St. Ignatius believed that we can find God in all things, at every moment, even in the most ordinary times. To do this, we must pay attention to what is happening in and around us and reflect on this experience. Ignatius encourages us to look back over a period of time and also to look ahead, to what comes next, so that we can act in a way worthy of who we are and who God calls us to be.

A daily practice of praying the Examen (about ten or fifteen minutes) helps us discern how God is calling us in small and large ways. God is found in what is real, so we pray from what is real in our lives. It is the most practical of prayers.

Over the centuries, the Examen has been adapted in many ways. Feel free to adapt the language or the practice of the Examen to where you are on your spiritual journey. I have broken down this daily prayer into five steps. In the spirit of adaptability, so vital to Ignatian spirituality, you do not need to do all five steps or use a precise formula of words. If one step in particular moves you on a day, stick with it.

What follows is a general overview of those five steps.

1. **Pray for God's Help**

   There is nothing magical about praying. Prayer is a conversation with God, by whatever name you call the Divine. Invite God to be with you during this sacred time. The Examen invites you to change perspective. Let yourself see your day as God sees it.

   Remember, Ignatius experienced a God who helped and encouraged him. In that spirit, ask God to help *you* be grateful and honest as you look back on the day and to be attentive to how God's Spirit was working in and through you, others, and creation.

2. **Give Thanks for the Gifts of This Day**

   For Ignatius, gratitude is a key step on the spiritual journey. An attitude of gratitude, practiced often enough, helps us find God in all things and can transform the way we look at our life and at other people. So, review the day and name the blessings, from the most significant and obvious to the more common and ordinary.

   God (*not* the devil) is found in the details, so be very specific! As you take stock, honor the gifts of others in your life, but do not forget to recognize the gifts in *you*, for they, too, are God-given.

   Do not feel that you must mechanically go through the day hour by hour or make a list of the day's gifts. Instead, savor whatever gifts God shows you. With God's gentle guidance, *let the day run through you*, rather than you running through the day.

3. **Pray over the Significant Interior Movements That Surface as You Replay the Day**

   Ignatius believed that God communicates with us not only through mental insight but also through our "interior movements," as he called them: thoughts, imaginings, emotions, inclinations, desires, feelings, repulsions, and attractions. As you reflect on the day, you may notice some strong feelings arise. They may be painful or pleasing—for example, joy, peace, sadness, anxiety, confusion, hope, compassion, regret, anger, confidence, jealousy, self-doubt, boredom, excitement.

Feelings are neither positive nor negative: it is what you do with them that raises moral questions. These movements can tell you about the direction of your life on this specific day. And simply bringing them to the surface can help release the destructive hold that some feelings have on you.

Pick one or two strong feelings or movements and pray from them. Ask: *Where did they come from and where did they lead?*

Did they draw you closer to God? Did they help you grow in faith, hope, and love? Did they make you more generous with your time and talent? Did they make you feel more alive, whole, and human? Did they lead you to feel more connected to others or challenge you to life-giving growth? *These are movements of consolation.*

Or did the feelings lead you away from God, make you less faithful, hopeful, and loving? Did they cause you to become more self-centered or anxious? Did they lure you into needless doubts and confusion? Did they lead to the breakdown of relationships? *These are movements of desolation.*

This is what Ignatius means by "discernment of spirits."

As in Ignatius's life, so in ours: we all have spiritual ups and downs. We become more spiritually wise by identifying patterns of consolation and desolation so that we can act out of consolation, and avoid acting in desolation.

4. **Rejoice and Seek Forgiveness**

   Rejoice in those times of consolation when you felt close to God and others and at peace with yourself. Ask for forgiveness for those times today when you resisted God's presence or when you were not your best self. Thank God for the grace of awareness given to you during this time of prayer, even if you became aware of things you are not proud of. This awareness is the beginning of healing and growth.

5. **Look to Tomorrow**

   Just as God is with you today, God will be with you as you sleep and when you wake up tomorrow. Invite God to be a part of your future.

*What do you need God's help with?* Be very practical and specific. If it's helpful, look at your schedule for tomorrow. God wants to be there with you, in the most dramatic and mundane moments of your day. Ask God to give you the grace you need—for example, courage, confidence, wisdom, patience, determination, or peace. Or perhaps there is someone you would like to pray for by name.

Close by speaking to God from your heart or with a prayer that is familiar to you, such as the Our Father.

# In Gratitude

For St. Ignatius, gratitude is one of the most important spiritual dispositions because it naturally opens us up to God and others and inspires our own generosity. I thus end this book with words of gratitude for some of the people who accompanied me on this adventure in writing.

*Seeing with the Heart* emerged out of a theology class I taught at Georgetown for many years. I am grateful for the many students who explored with me fundamental questions like those addressed here. They did so with such sincerity, creativity, generosity, and courage.

I thank my provincial superior, Joseph O'Keefe, SJ, for his personal support and for giving me a sabbatical (my first as a Jesuit) to write the book, which I tried unsuccessfully to do while working full-time in the years before. During my sabbatical, I was blessed to live and work at the America House Jesuit Community in Manhattan. Thanks to my Jesuit brothers there who encouraged and supported me during my time with them. They also provided many happy diversions when I needed them!

When I finished a draft, my Jesuit brothers Gerry Blaszczak, SJ, Mark Ravizza, SJ, Jim McDermott, SJ, my friend and fellow author Tim Shriver, and former student and now friend Margaret Delaney, provided invaluable and insightful feedback and helped me bring together the various themes into a cohesive whole. For additional feedback, I also shared the draft with other former students who, like Margaret, took the class that generated this book: Lizzy Macgill, Joaquin Pannunzio, and Tyler Sanborn.

Special thanks to Yamiche Alcindor, Clint Morrison, Kurt Denk, and Susan Pattillo for helping me craft some of the book's narrative.

I am grateful for the gentle and persistent encouragement of my friends at Loyola Press to write a second book, following *The Ignatian Adventure* (2011). Particular thanks to Gary Jansen, who shepherded the project, and to Vinita Wright, who edited my manuscript with great care and expertise (as she did for my first book).

Doing theology is deeply personal, as it touches on matters of faith and on some of the most important questions of human life. Traveling this distance between head and heart has not always been easy for me, but I was blessed to have dear friends and mentors who helped me along the way. In the year of sabbatical writing this book, I especially wish to acknowledge: Sr. Sandy Bay, SSND, Greg Bonfiglio, SJ, Greg Boyle, SJ, the Brosnan family, Alma Caballero, Nancy Calcagnini, Luis Calero, SJ, Marcia Chatelain, the Connor family, Emily Deyoung, Anne Dinkelspiel, Chris and Jordan Duffner, Peter Etzel, SJ, Ken Gavin, SJ, Tim Kesicki, SJ, Lisa Kloppenberg, the Lenihan family, Jeanne Lord, Doug Marcoullier, SJ, Jim Martin, SJ, John McGarry, SJ, the McGrath family, Mike Meaney and Lizette Valles, Stephanie Moergen, the O'Malley family, John Privett, SJ, Ed Quinn, Bill Rewak, SJ, A.J. Rizzo, SJ, the Rooney family, Jeanne, Matt, and Jenae Ruesch, Margaret Russell, Jim Shea, SJ, the Skonberg family, Greg Smith, the Smulson family, Kevin and Alyssa Sullivan, Jack Treacy, SJ, Jill and Chris Welsh, George Witt, SJ, and Michael Zampelli, SJ.

Throughout the book, I share important moments in my family's history. My sister Cathy and brother Andy have put up with me for many decades and have shaped the best parts of me. Their spouses, Tom and Wendy, have made my life all the better. And to Jack and Elizabeth, I could not be prouder of the persons you have become and can only hope that what I share here will be of help to you and your generation as you navigate life's adventures, so full of promise.

Finally, as in all things, so this book: to God goes the glory, *Ad Majorem Dei Gloriam.*

# Sources

**Page xiii:** Pope Francis, *Evangelii Gaudium: On the Proclamation of the Gospel in Today's World* (2013), 6. https://www.vatican.va/content/ francesco/en/apost_exhortations/documents/ papa-francesco_esortazione-ap_20131124_evangelii-gaudium.html (abbreviated as EG, followed by paragraph number).

**Page 2:** C. P. Cavafy, "Ithaka," trans. Edmund Keeley, in *C. P. Cavafy: Collected Poems* (Princeton, NJ: Princeton University Press, 1975). https://www.poetryfoundation.org/poems/51296/ithaka-56d22eef917ec.

**Page 3:** Pema Chödrön, *When Things Fall Apart: Heart Advice for Difficult Times* (Boston: Shambhala Publications, 2000) 66.

**Page 3:** T.S. Eliot, *Four Quartets* (New York: Harcourt, Inc., 1971) 39.

**Page 6:** Joseph N. Tylenda, *A Pilgrim's Journey: The Autobiography of Ignatius of Loyola* (Collegeville, MN: Liturgical Press, 1991). (Abbreviated as *Autobiography*, followed by section number).

**Page 10:** Arturo Sosa, *Walking with Ignatius* (Chicago: Loyola Press, 2021) 125.

**Page 12:** *Lady Bird* (2017). Greta Gerwig, director. Production companies: IAC Films, Scott Rudin Productions, Entertainment 360. https://www.youtube.com/watch?v=GUo2XuqMcCU.

**Page 12:** Pádraig Ó Tuama, *In the Shelter: Finding a Home in the World* (Minneapolis: Broadleaf Books, 2015) 73.

**Page 12:** David Foster Wallace, *This Is Water: Some Thoughts, Delivered on a Significant Occasion, about Living a Compassionate Life* (New York: Little, Brown and Co., 2009) 3–4.

**Page 13:** Ibid., 92–93.

**Page 14:** Saint-Exupery quoted in Joan Chittister, *Between the Dark and the Daylight: Embracing the Contradictions of Life* (New York: Image, 2015) 159.

**Page 14:** Jonathan Montaldo, ed., *A Year with Thomas Merton: Daily Meditations from His Journals* (New York: HarperOne, 2004) 315.

**Page 20:** Elie Wiesel, *Night*, trans. Marion Wiesel (New York: Hill and Wang, 2006) 4–5.

**Page 20:** Monika K. Hellwig, *Understanding Catholicism*, 2nd ed. (New York: Paulist Press, 2002) 1.

**Page 23:** Karl Rahner, *Foundations of Christian Faith: An Introduction to the Idea of Christianity*, trans. William V. Dych, SJ (New York: Crossroad, 1999) 32, 65–66.

**Page 23:** John O'Donohue, *Walking in Wonder: Eternal Wisdom for a Modern World*, interview with John Quinn (New York: Convergent, 2015) 6.

**Page 26:** Wiesel, *Night*, 5.

**Page 26:** Hellwig, *Understanding Catholicism*, 4.

**Page 27:** Ibid.

**Page 29:** Anne Lamott, *Bird by Bird: Some Instructions on Writing and Life* (New York: Anchor Books, 2019) 29.

**Page 30:** *Autobiography*, sect. 27.

**Page 31:** Pope Francis, *A Big Heart Open to God: A Conversation with Pope Francis*, interview with Antonio Spadaro (New York: HarperOne, 2013) 48.

**Page 32:** Heschel quoted in Michael J. Buckley, *What Do You Seek? The Questions of Jesus as Challenge and Promise* (Grand Rapids, MI: William B. Eerdmans Publishing, 2016) xi.

**Page 32:** Rainer Maria Rilke, *Letters to a Young Poet* (Merchant Books, 2012) 30–31.

**Page 34:** Brian Grogan, *God Is Right in Front of You: A Field Guide to Ignatian Spirituality* (Chicago: Loyola Press, 2021) 98.

**Page 34:** Gregory Boyle, *The Whole Language: The Power of Extravagant Tenderness* (New York: Avid Reader Press, 2021) 4.

**Page 37:** Thomas Merton, *Conjectures of a Guilty Bystander* (Garden City, NY: Image Books, 1968) 156, 158.

**Page 38:** Alice Walker, *The Color Purple* (Penguin Books, 2019) 195–96.

**Page 39:** Gerard Manley Hopkins, "Hurrahing in Harvest," in *Gerard Manley Hopkins: Poems and Prose* (New York: Penguin Classics, 1985). https://hopkinspoetry.com/poem/hurrahing-in-harvest/.

**Page 39:** Pope Francis, *Big Heart Open to God*, 50.

**Page 40:** *Autobiography*, sect. 11.

**Page 40:** Wendell Berry, "The Peace of Wild Things." https://onbeing.org/poetry/the-peace-of-wild-things/.

**Page 41:** Gerard Manley Hopkins, "God's Grandeur," in *Gerard Manley Hopkins: Poems and Prose* (New York: Penguin Classics, 1985). https://www.poetryfoundation.org/poems/44395/gods-grandeur.

**Page 41:** Pierre Teilhard de Chardin, *The Divine Milieu: An Essay on the Interior Life* (London: William Collins Sons & Co., 1960) 99–100.

**Page 42:** Nicholas Carr, *The Shallows: What the Internet Is Doing to Our Brains* (New York: W.W. Norton & Co., 2011) 7.

**Page 42:** Browning quoted at https://www.bartleby.com/236/86.html.

**Page 42:** Joyce quoted in John Sexton, *Baseball as a Road to God: Seeing Beyond the Game* (New York: Gotham Books, 2013) 212.

**Page 43:** *Chariots of Fire* (1981). Hugh Hudson. Production companies: Enigma Productions, Allied Stars, Ltd. (U.S., Warner Brothers). https://www.youtube.com/watch?v=Pd5LCN53q9Y

**Page 45:** *Autobiography*, sect. 30.

**Page 45:** Thích Nhât Hanh, *The Miracle of Mindfulness: An Introduction to the Practice of Meditation*, trans. Mobi Ho (Boston: Beacon Press, 1987) 3–5.

**Page 46:** Walter J. Burghardt, "Contemplation: A Long Loving Look at the Real," in George W. Traub, ed., *An Ignatian Spirituality Reader: Contemporary Writings on St. Ignatius of Loyola, the Spiritual Exercises, Discernment, and More* (Chicago: Loyola Press, 2008) 89–98.

**Page 47:** Antoine de Saint-Exupéry, *The Little Prince*, trans. Richard Howard (New York: Harcourt, 2000) 63, 59, 64.

**Page 48:** Ibid., 60.

**Page 48:** Timothy Radcliffe, *Why Go To Church? The Drama of the Eucharist* (New York: Continuum, 2008) 150.

**Page 50:** Anne Lamott, *Dusk, Night, Dawn: On Revival and Courage* (New York: Riverhead Books, 2021) 169.

**Page 50:** Gregory Boyle, *Barking to the Choir: The Power of Radical Kinship* (New York: Simon & Schuster, 2017) 136.

**Page 52:** Pope Francis, *Lumen fidei: On Faith* (2013) 4. https://www.vatican.va/content/francesco/en/encyclicals/documents/papa-francesco_20130629_enciclica-lumen-fidei.html.

**Page 54:** Michael J. Himes, *The Mystery of Faith: An Introduction to Catholicism* (Cincinnati, OH: St. Anthony Messenger Press, 2004) 17–18.

**Page 56:** *Field of Dreams* (1989). Director: Phil Alden Robinson. Producer: Gordon Company. Distributer: Universal Pictures. https://www.youtube.com/watch?v=izF0LoBkhZY.

**Page 59:** *Autobiography*, sect. 1.

**Page 60:** Ibid., 7–8, 11. See also Comerford, *The Pilgrim's Story: The Life and Spirituality of St. Ignatius Loyola* (Chicago: Loyola Press, 2017) 11–16.

**Page 61:** Sosa, *Walking with Ignatius*, 5, xv.

**Page 62:** Garden analogy inspired by Wayne Muller, *Sabbath: Finding Rest, Renewal, and Delight in our Busy Lives* (New York: Bantam Books, 2000) 142.

**Page 63:** Frankl, 65–66, 37–38.

**Page 65:** James F. Keenan, *Moral Wisdom: Lessons and Texts from the Catholic Tradition* (New York: Rowman & Littlefield Publishers, 2004) 57.

**Page 67:** For beautiful, extended meditation on the parable, see Henri J. M. Nouwen, *The Return of the Prodigal Son: A Story of Homecoming* (New York: Image Books, 1994).

**Page 70:** Dante reference found in Himes, *Mystery of Faith*, 32.

**Page 70:** Luther quoted in N. T. Wright, *Broken Signposts: How Christianity Makes Sense of the World* (New York: HarperOne, 2020) 127.

**Page 70:** Richard Rohr, *Breathing under Water: Spirituality and the Twelve Steps* (Cincinnati, OH: St. Anthony Messenger Press, 2011) 95.

**Page 71:** James Alison, "Blindsided by God: Reconciliation from the Underside," *Presentation for "Anatomy of Reconciliation" Conference, Trinity Institute, New York City, 30 January–1 Feb 2006.* http://jamesalison.com/blindsided-by-god/.

**Page 72:** O Tuama, *In the Shelter*, 190.

**Page 72:** For biblical references to fear, see Richard Rohr, *Falling Upward: A Spirituality for the Two Halves of Life* (San Francisco: Jossey-Bass, 2011) 6;

Peter van Breemen, *The God of Our Deepest Longings: Seven Biblical Meditations*, trans. Peter Heinegg (Notre Dame, IN: Ave Maria Press, 2009) 102.

**Page 73:** Amanda Gorman, "Why I Almost Didn't Read My Poem at the Inauguration," *New York Times*, January 20, 2022, https://www.nytimes.com/2022/01/20/opinion/ amanda-gorman-poem-inauguration.html.

**Page 74:** Radcliffe, *Why Go to Church*, 21.

**Page 74:** Himes, *Mystery of Faith*, 29–30, 35.

**Page 74:** Karl Rahner, *The Need and Blessing of Prayer: A New Translation of Father Rahner's Book on Prayer*, trans. Bruce W. Gillette (Collegeville, MN: Liturgical Press, 1997) 6–8.

**Page 75:** Pope Francis, *A Big Heart Open to God*, 8–9.

**Page 76:** Vincent quoted in Ernest Kurtz and Katherine Ketcham, *The Spirituality of Imperfection: Storytelling and the Search for Meaning* (New York: Bantam Books, 2002) 1.

**Page 76:** Montaldo, *A Year with Thomas Merton*, 106.

**Page 77:** Gorman, https://www.nytimes.com/2022/01/20/opinion/ amanda-gorman-poem-inauguration.html.

**Page 77:** Chödrön, *When Things Fall Apart*, 2.

**Page 77:** *Alcoholics Anonymous: The Story of How Many Thousands of Men and Women Have Recovered from Alcoholism*, 4th ed. (New York: Alcoholics Anonymous World Services, 2001) 59.

**Page 78:** Wallace, *This is Water*, 98-102, 120-21.

**Page 79:** Pope Francis, *Sharing the Wisdom of Time*, ed. Rosemary Lane and Tom McGrath (Chicago: Loyola Press, 2018) 11.

**Page 84:** Rilke, *Letters to a Young Poet*, 14–15.

**Page 84:** Timothy Radcliffe, *Seven Last Words* (New York: Burns & Oates, 2004) 51–52.

**Page 84:** Ignatius of Loyola, "Letter to Jean Pelletier," June 12, 1551. https://library.georgetown.edu/woodstock/ignatius-letters/ letter17#footnotes. See also Edward Kinerk, "Eliciting Great Desires: Their Place in the Spirituality of the Society of Jesus," *Studies in the Spirituality of Jesuits* 16, no. 5 (1984). https://ejournals.bc.edu/index.php/ jesuit/article/view/3730.

**Page 86:** Thomas Aquinas, *Summa Theologica*, trans. Fathers of the English Dominican Province (Benziger Brothers, 1947) IIaIIae.129.3 ad 4. https://www.ccel.org/a/aquinas/summa/home.html.

**Page 87:** For references to AMDG in Constitutions, see Avery Dulles, "What Distinguishes the Jesuits," *America*, January 15, 2007. https://www.americamagazine.org/faith/2007/01/15/what-distinguishes-jesuits.

**Page 87:** For more background on the *magis*, see Barton T. Geger, "What Magis Really Means and Why It Matters," *Jesuit Higher Education: A Journal* 1, no. 2 (2012). https://epublications.regis.edu/jhe/vol1/iss2/16/.

**Page 87:** 34th General Congregation of the Society of Jesus, Decree 26 (1995) nn. 26–27. https://jesuitportal.bc.edu/research/documents/1995_decree26gc34/.

**Page 91:** Theodore Roosevelt, "Citizenship in a Republic" (address at the Sorbonne), April 23, 1910. https://www.theodorerooseveltcenter.org/Learn-About-TR/TR-Encyclopedia/Culture-and-Society/Man-in-the-Arena.aspx.

**Page 100:** Augustine quoted in Peter van Breemen, *The God Who Won't Let Go* (Notre Dame, IN: Ave Maria Press, 2006) 147–48.

**Page 100:** Radcliffe, *Why Go to Church*, 95.

**Page 101:** John Dearden, "Prophets of a Future Not Our Own" (homily), October 25, 1979. https://www.usccb.org/prayer-and-worship/prayers-and-devotions/prayers/prophets-of-a-future-not-our-own.

**Page 103:** For more on the virtue of humility and magnanimity, see William McCormick, "A Continual Sacrifice to the Glory of God: Ignatian Magnanimity as Cooperation with the Divine," *Studies in the Spirituality of Jesuits* 50, no. 3 (2018) 15–34. https://ejournals.bc.edu/index.php/jesuit/article/view/10906.

**Page 104:** Matt Emerson, "Pope Francis: Teaching to be 'Great Souled,'" *America*, January 28, 2014. https://www.americamagazine.org/content/ignatian-educator/pope-francis-teaching-be-great-souled.

**Page 104:** Cardinal Nguyen van Thuan quoted in Pope Francis, *Gaudete et exsultate: On the Call to Holiness in Today's World* (2018) 17. https://www.vatican.va/content/francesco/en/apost_exhortations/documents/papa-francesco_esortazione-ap_20180319_gaudete-et-exsultate.html (abbreviated GE).

**Page 105:** Simone Weil to Joë Bousquet, April 13, 1942; Simone Pétrement, *Simone Weil: A Life* (1976), trans. Raymond Rosenthal, in *Oxford Essential Quotations* (4th ed.) Susan Ratcliffe, ed. (Oxford: Oxford University Press, 2016).

**Page 105:** George Eliot, *Middlemarch*. ed. David Carroll (Oxford: Clarendon Press, 1986) 825.

**Page 106:** Timothy Shriver, *Fully Alive: Discovering What Matters Most* (New York: Sarah Crichton Books, 2014) 23–24, 36-37. For more information on Special Olympics, see https://www.specialolympics.org.

**Page 107:** Ibid., 250.

**Page 109:** John R. Donahue and Daniel J. Harrington, *The Gospel of Mark*, Sacra Pagina Series vol. 2, ed. Daniel J. Harrington (Collegeville, MN: Liturgical Press, 2005) 2:205, n. 34.

**Page 109:** M. Shawn Copeland, *Knowing Christ Crucified: The Witness of African American Religious Experience* (Maryknoll, NY: Orbis Books, 2018) 143.

**Page 111:** For biblical use of *agape*, see John Painter, *1, 2, and 3 John*, Sacra Pagina Series, vol. 18, ed. Daniel J. Harrington (Collegeville, MN: Liturgical Press, 2002) 18:170, n. 5; 265–66, nn. 7–8.

**Page 111:** For different meanings of love, see Himes, *Mystery of Faith*, 6, 8.

**Page 112:** Maria Popova, "John Steinbeck on Falling in Love: A 1958 Letter," *The Atlantic*, January 13, 2012. https://www.theatlantic.com/entertainment/archive/2012/01/john-steinbeck-on-falling-in-love-a-1958-letter/251375/.

**Page 112:** Laura Wamsley and Emily Sullivan, "Juan Romero, Busboy Who Cradled Dying RFK, Dies at 68," *NPR*, October 4, 2018. https://www.npr.org/2018/10/04/654282422/juan-romero-busboy-who-cradled-dying-rfk-dies-at-68.

**Page 113:** Óscar Romero in James R. Brockman, ed. and trans., *Óscar Romero: The Violence of Love* (Maryknoll, NY: Orbis Books, 2004) 175.

**Page 113:** Michael Himes, "A Lesson in Love" (2016). https://www.youtube.com/watch?v=gtUM6UYPRRY. Poster: Church in the 21st Century, Boston College. October 5, 2016. Length 3:44.

**Page 115:** Henry Ossawa Tanner, *The Annunciation* (1898), Philadelphia Museum of Art. https://philamuseum.org/collection/object/104384.

**Page 116:** Second Vatican Council, *Gaudium et spes: Pastoral Constitution on the Church in the Modern World* (1965) 22. https://www.vatican.va/archive/

hist_councils/ii_vatican_council/documents/
vat-ii_const_19651207_gaudium-et-spes_en.html.

**Page 116:** O'Donohue, *Walking in Wonder*, 20.

**Page 117:** Pope Francis, *The Church of Mercy: A Vision for the Church* (Chicago: Loyola Press, 2014) 138.

**Page 118:** For reflection on parable of the good Samaritan, see Pope Francis, *Fratelli tutti: On Fraternity and Social Friendship* (2020) https://www.vatican.va/content/francesco/en/encyclicals/documents/papa-francesco_20201003_enciclica-fratelli-tutti.html. (Abbreviated FT).

**Page 118:** Gerald O'Collins, *Pause for Thought: Making Time for Prayer, Jesus, and God* (New York: Paulist Press, 2011) 57.

**Page 119:** Amor Towles, *The Lincoln Highway* (New York: Viking, 2021) 132.

**Page 120:** Tuama, *In the Shelter*, 92.

**Page 120:** Pope Francis, *Laudato si': On Care for Our Common Home* (2015) 89. https://www.vatican.va/content/francesco/en/encyclicals/documents/papa-francesco_20150524_enciclica-laudato-si.html. (Abbreviated LS)

**Page 121:** For insightful reflection on mutuality in ministry, see Henri J. M. Nouwen, *Gracias: A Latin American Journal* (Maryknoll, NY: Orbis, 1999) 19.

**Page 122:** For more information on Homeboy Industries, see https://homeboyindustries.org/.

**Page 123:** Gregory Boyle, *Tattoos on the Heart: The Power of Boundless Compassion* (New York: Free Press, 2010) 188, 172.

**Page 123:** John Leland, "Sister Elaine Roulet, 89, Dies; Aided Imprisoned Mothers and Their Children," *New York Times*, August 24, 2020, https://www.nytimes.com/2020/08/22/nyregion/sister-elaine-roulet-dead.html.

**Page 125:** Sobrino, *Principle of Mercy*, 10.

**Page 125:** Nikita Stewart, "'I've Been to the Mountaintop': Dr. King's Last Sermon Annotated," *New York Times*, April 2, 2018. https://www.nytimes.com/interactive/2018/04/02/us/king-mlk-last-sermon-annotated.html.

**Page 126:** Boyle, *Tattoos*, 190.

**Page 126:** Boyle, *Barking to the Choir*, 165.

**Page 127:** C. S. Lewis, *The Four Loves* (New York: Harcourt, Brace & Co., 1988) 121.

**Page 128:** Boyle, *Tattoos*, 72.

**Page 128:** Romero, pastoral letter, in Kevin Clarke, *Oscar Romero: Love Must Win Out* (Collegeville, MN: Liturgical Press, 2014) 120.

**Page 128:** Romero, in Clarke, 111.

**Page 129:** Dorothy Day, *All the Way to Heaven: The Selected Letters of Dorothy Day*, ed. Robert Ellsberg (Milwaukee: Marquette University Press, 2010) 220.

**Page 129:** Joel Lovell, "George Saunders's Advice to Graduates," *6th Floor* (blog), *New York Times*, July 31, 2013, https://6thfloor.blogs.nytimes.com/2013/07/31/george-saunderss-advice-to-graduates/.

**Page 130:** Boyle, *Whole Language*, 180.

**Page 130:** Boyle, *Barking to the Choir*, 51.

**Page 130:** Chödrön, *When Things Fall Apart*, 140.

**Page 131:** "How a Rejected Block of Marble Became the World's Most Famous Statue," *Encyclopaedia Britannica*, https://www.britannica.com/story/how-a-rejected-block-of-marble-became-the-worlds-most-famous-statue.

**Page 135:** John O'Donohue, *To Bless the Space Between Us: A Book of Blessings* (New York: Doubleday, 2008) 117.

**Page 136:** Matt Miller, "*WandaVision* Episode 8's Quote about Grief Has Become the Show's Defining Moment," *Esquire*, March 3, 2021. https://www.esquire.com/entertainment/tv/a35713623/wandavision-episode-8-grief-quote-explained/.

**Page 138:** For explanation of law of retribution, see Daniel Harrington, *Why Do We Suffer? A Scriptural Approach to the Human Condition* (Franklin, WI: Sheed & Ward, 2000) 15–16.

**Page 142:** Jon Sobrino, *Where Is God? Earthquake, Terrorism, Barbarity, and Hope*, trans. Margaret Wilde (Maryknoll, NY: Orbis Books, 2004) 150.

**Page 143:** Copeland, *Knowing Christ Crucified*, 25, 26.

**Page 144:** Eliot, *Four Quartets*, 28.

**Page 144:** O'Donohue, *Walking in Wonder*, 94, 121–22.

**Page 145:** Alexander Pope, "An Essay on Man: Epistle I," https://www.poetryfoundation.org/poems/44899/an-essay-on-man-epistle-i.

**Page 145:** Richard Rohr, "Transforming Pain," *Center for Action and Contemplation* (blog), October 17, 2018, https://cac.org/daily-meditations/transforming-pain-2018-10-17/.

**Page 145:** Kennedy quoted in: https://www.jfklibrary.org/learn/about-jfk/the-kennedy-family/robert-f-kennedy/robert-f-kennedy-speeches/statement-on-assassination-of-martin-luther-king-jr-indianapolis-indiana-april-4-1968.

**Page 146:** Dag Hammarskjold quoted in Gerald O'Collins, *Pause for Thought* (New York: Paulist Press, 2011) 80.

**Page 147:** O'Donohue, *Bless the Space between Us*, 107.

**Page 147:** Nikita Stewart, "'I've Been to the Mountaintop': Dr. King's Last Sermon Annotated," *New York Times*, April 2, 2018, https://www.nytimes.com/interactive/2018/04/02/us/king-mlk-last-sermon-annotated.html.

**Page 148:** Dickinson quoted in Timothy Radcliffe, *What Is the Point of Being a Christian?* (New York: Burns & Oats, 2005) 28.

**Page 148:** Havel quoted in Radcliffe, *What Is the Point of Being a Christian?*, 17.

**Page 148:** Frankl, *Man's Search for Meaning*, 67.

**Page 148:** Radcliffe, *What Is the Point of Being a Christian?*, 23.

**Page 148:** For more information on the Equal Justice Initiative and the National Memorial for Peace and Justice, see https://museumandmemorial.eji.org/memorial

**Page 148:** Bryan Stevenson, interview by Krista Tippett, *On Being* (podcast), episode no. 1,003 (November 4, 2021). https://onbeing.org/programs/bryan-stevenson-finding-the-courage-for-whats-redemptive/#transcript.

**Page 149:** John Cary, "'This Is Sacred Ground': A Visit to the Lynching Memorial in Alabama," Ideas.Ted.com, May 4, 2018, https://ideas.ted.com/this-is-sacred-ground-a-visit-to-the-lynching-memorial-in-alabama/. For the website of Equal Justice Initiative, National Memorial for Peace and Justice, see https://museumandmemorial.eji.org/memorial.

**Page 149:** N. T. Wright, *Surprised by Hope: Rethinking Heaven, the Resurrection, and the Mission of the Church* (New York: HarperOne, 2008) 50.

**Page 150:** For understanding of resurrection in ancient Judaism and early Christianity, see Wright, *Surprised by Hope*, 35–51.

**Page 150:** For understanding of resurrection as new creation, see N. T. Wright, *Christians at the Cross: Finding Hope in the Passion, Death, and Resurrection of Jesus* (Ijamsville, MD: The Word among Us Press, 2007) 75; Wright, *Surprised by Hope*, 96, 259.

**Page 150:** Wright, *Surprised by Hope*, 255, 293.

**Page 151:** Ibid., 19.

**Page 151:** Emily Dickinson, *The Complete Poems of Emily Dickinson* (Boston: Little, Brown and Co., 1924), https://www.bartleby.com/113/1100.html.

**Page 154:** Margaret Silf, *The Other Side of Chaos: Breaking Through When Life Is Breaking Down* (Chicago: Loyola Press, 2011) 65.

**Page 154:** Kubler-Ross quoted in Joyce Rupp, *Boundless Compassion: Creating a Way of Life* (Notre Dame, IN: Sorin Books, 2018) 182.

**Page 160:** For a helpful overview of the Rules for Discernment, see Michael Ivens, *Understanding the Spiritual Exercises: Text and Commentary* (Herefordshire, UK: Gracewing, 1998) 205–237.

**Page 161:** Pope Francis, *Let Us Dream: The Path to a Better Future* (New York: Simon and Schuster, 2020) 21.

**Page 163:** *Autobiography*, 8.

**Page 164:** Mark E. Thibodeaux, *Ignatian Discernment of Spirits in Spiritual Direction and Pastoral Care: Going Deeper* (Chicago: Loyola Press, 2020) 26.

**Page 167:** Mark E. Thibodeaux, *God's Voice Within: The Ignatian Way to Discover God's Will* (Chicago: Loyola Press, 2010) 22–23.

**Page 168:** David L. Fleming, *Draw Me into Your Friendship: The Spiritual Exercises—A Literal Translation and a Contemporary Reading* (St. Louis, MO: Institute of Jesuit Sources, 1996) 255.

**Page 168:** Ibid., 257, 259.

**Page 177:** Gerard Manley Hopkins, "As Kingfishers Catch Fire," in *Gerard Manley Hopkins: Poems and Prose* (New York: Penguin Classics, 1985). https://www.poetryfoundation.org/poems/44389/as-kingfishers-catch-fire.

**Page 177:** Frederick Buechner, *Wishful Thinking: A Theological ABC* (New York: Harper and Row, 1973) 95.

**Page 177:** Himes, *Mystery of Faith*, 77–78.

**Page 177:** *The Constitutions of the Society of Jesus and Their Complementary Norms: A Complete English Translation of Official Latin Texts*, trans. George E. Ganss (St. Louis, MO: Institute of Jesuit Sources, 1996) 622.

**Page 179:** Pope Francis, *Let Us Dream*, 21, 51.

**Page 180:** Ibid., 54.

**Page 180:** For the need to exercise discernment in complicated pastoral situations, see Pope Francis, *Amoris laetitia: On Love in the Family* (2016) 308. https://www.vatican.va/content/francesco/en/apost_exhortations/documents/papa-francesco_esortazione-ap_20160319_amoris-laetitia.html 304–312.

**Page 181:** *Autobiography*, 46–47, 96.

**Page 181:** Pope Francis, *Big Heart Open to God*, 49.

**Page 181:** See "Jazz Music Explained: How to Play, Listen to, and Enjoy Jazz Music for Beginners!" https://www.youtube.com/watch?v=StM6blsh-Xg. Presenter: Dean Demarzo. Poster: Paul Effman Music Store. Date: May 23, 2020. Length: 7:08.

**Page 185:** Odysseus ending inspired by Rohr, *Falling Upward*, xxxii.

**Page 185:** Alfred, Lord Tennyson, "Ulysses," https://www.poetryfoundation.org/poems/45392/ulysses.

**Page 186:** "Fra Giovanni Giocondo," Britannica.com, https://www.britannica.com/biography/Fra-Giovanni-Giocondo.

**Page 186:** Fra Giovanni, "A Letter to the Most Illustrious the Contessina Allagia Dela Aldobrandeschi, Written Christmas Eve Anno Domini 1513," https://www.bartleby.com/73/1467.html.

**Page 187:** David Brooks, *The Road to Character* (New York: Random House, 2016) xi.

**Page 187:** Romero, *Violence of Love*, 119.

**Page 188:** Dorothy Day, *The Long Loneliness* (San Francisco: HarperSanFrancisco, 1981) 285–86.

# About the Author

Kevin O'Brien, SJ, is a former lawyer who became a Jesuit more than 25 years ago. He regularly conducts spiritual retreats for the young and old alike. An experienced high school teacher and college professor, he is the author of *The Ignatian Adventure*.